Reasonably
THIN

Reasonably THIN

JESSE DILLINGER

THOMAS NELSON PUBLISHERS
Nashville

Published in Nashville, Tennessee, by Thomas Nelson, Inc.

Library of Congress Cataloging-in-Publication Data

Dillinger, Jesse.
    Reasonably thin : spiritual aspects of over- and undereating / Jesse
Dillinger.
        p.   cm.
    ISBN 0-7852-7062-0 (pbk.)
    1. Eating disorders—Patients—Religious life. 2. Eating disorders—
Religious aspects—Christianity. I. Title.
BV4910.35.D55   1998
616.85'2606—dc21
                                                            98-16303
                                                            CIP

Printed in the United States of America
3 4 5 6 7 8 9 10 — 02 01 00 99 98

I turned to God and, in obedience, worked with Him as He led me out of the depths of sin and pain. Then, I turned to Him to lead me out of the tenacious struggle with weight. This book and my being reasonably thin are the result.

Jesse A. Dillinger, M.A., MFCC

Contents

Acknowledgments

God has been so good to me, lifting me out of sin and shame, reviving me in His love and mercy! It amazes me that He would give me such good friends to support me and encourage me on this long road to publication.

There is Beverly who has been such a wonderful friend and model of faithfulness to the Lord. I share her fierce determination to serve Him and am so grateful that the Lord has blessed me by allowing us to serve together. I could never thank her enough for her support and encouragement. Often I have said to her when it comes to her heart for the Lord, "I want to be just like you!"

There are Bev and Mary, to whom I have been accountable and by whom I have been led. Their friendship and support mean a great deal to me.

John took a personal interest in my work and has been a great encouragement to me. Words cannot express my gratitude. May God multiply His blessings to him.

And how can I thank Ernest and Pauline? With the exception of very few others, never have two people so faithfully believed in me and my desire to serve the Lord. Their devotion to Him, to me, to this book, and to my career could never be repaid. I hereby adopt them. They are now Ernie and Pauline Dillinger!

There are others too—Lorie, Don, Joy, Nancy, and Julie who prayed for me and supported me before and during this work. Lois and Ethel have been praying for me from the beginning. Dottie was used of the Lord to reopen the doors of service. And there are a handful of very significant others, not mentioned here due to confidentiality issues, who were praying for me in the last days of writing this book. I thank them too.

In this project, I have lived with others the life and fellowship of the body of Christ as He would have it be. I thank God for that. I thank God for His Son, Jesus Christ, and I look forward to His return. To Him be maximum glory!

Note to the Reader

Because the information in this book contains truths that apply to both Christians and non-Christians alike, both will be reading this book. I welcome that. I will keep in mind that nonbelievers may also be reading the text. I will take care to respect them here and to be as clear as I can on their behalf. I welcome Christians and non-Christians to the journey into freedom.

The principles in this book go far beyond the topic. I encourage the reader to use them in as broad-based a fashion as each principle will allow.

Although stories in this book are based on actual incidents, names and details of the stories have been changed to protect privacy.

The information provided in this book is in no way intended to be a substitute for professional counseling. All individuals who are dealing with overeating or undereating, or are in any way altering their eating behavior, are encouraged to do so under the supervision of a physician, and, if necessary, seek psychological counseling. *Reasonably Thin* is not a diet book or a weight-loss program. *Reasonably Thin* does not address genetic or medical aspects of weight or psychiatric conditions related to weight. Any principles or recommendations in this book should be viewed by those who have genetic or medical issues with weight in light of and in respect to those conditions. Determining what foods are healthy is a subject left to individuals and their own nutritional specialists, and is not the subject of this book.

Preface

I am a Christian in private practice in San Diego, California, as a licensed Marriage, Family, and Child Counselor, with a practice devoted predominantly to Christians. I do treat some non-Christians. In my practice I have encountered a number of men and women who struggle with weight issues that range from formal eating disorders to issues of weight in general.

I will be providing information related to the spiritual aspects of overeating and undereating. By *spiritual* I mean that the principles will be drawn from the Bible, which I believe to be the infallible Word of God—the definitive text of the Christian life. I will also bring in psychological information as I think it relevant, and exercises to sharpen awareness. Most of this information is applicable to both Christians and non-Christians.

There are prayers at the end of each chapter of the book. I want to encourage you, as you read each chapter, to make a copy of that particular prayer and carry it with you. Referring to the prayer throughout the day is a great way to stay focused.

Once you are firmly grounded in the underlying foundation of *Reasonably Thin*, which is found in the earlier chapters, the remaining chapters will show you how it all works. You will find that *Reasonably Thin* is a book you will want to reference now and in years to come. This book is intended to encourage you in many more areas than just your struggle with weight. My prayer is that, in reading this book and following its guidelines, God will bless you abundantly, above and beyond all you have ever hoped for!

Introduction

In my practice as a Marriage, Family, and Child Counselor, it has been extremely painful for me to watch people who, in an attempt to find the miracle cure, look beyond the answer. They look beyond the gospel to other religions, beyond God's power to recovery programs, beyond His truth to believing in someone or something else.

It is not enough to call this the cardinal error of our time. It is the cardinal sin. Unless we see it as such, we will give up more than we will ever want to know we have given up when we see Him face-to-face. It is then that we will be held accountable for our own wood, hay, and stubble. Or we will receive the rewards associated with exercising our faith. The moment Christians move beyond faith, they move into the area of the flesh. The moment the non-Christian rejects exercising faith in Jesus Christ, they move beyond the truth and the only lasting answer.

I would have us stand still, here and now, and use what we have available to us. For non-Christians, I would have them stand where they are and receive Jesus Christ as Savior and Lord and start from there. At that point they are equipped, as all Christians are, to deal with any and all issues in life. That includes our struggles with weight.

No matter where you are in your spiritual journey, I encourage you to come along with me. Share with me the experience of soaring beyond dieting. Come along with me and learn to live free from bondage to food.

*"Therefore, whether you eat or drink, or whatever you do,
do all to the glory of God."*

1 Corinthians 10:31

1

You're
Not Alone

I used to be almost always uncomfortable going to the mall. I felt so self-conscious. I didn't look up at other people because I didn't want to see them looking at me. So I tended to walk with my eyes down. I'm surprised that I never walked into a wall! I did, however, find money on the ground from time to time. Being rewarded in this way kept me from looking up for a substantial number of years! Essentially, though, I was avoiding people. But it sounded better to me if I just referred to myself as an entrepreneur.

I felt physically and emotionally uncomfortable being overweight. One day, in feelings of frustration and hopelessness, I sat on a bench in the center of the mall. As my eyes began to cautiously drift upward, I began to see that people weren't looking at me. And I began to see something else: I was not the only one with a weight problem.

The next time you're in a mall, find a bench and sit down for a while. Watch people. Ask yourself, "Do most of these people seem reasonably thin?" Government studies will tell you the answer is no. Many of the people you see will weigh too much or too little.

Now ask yourself, "How do I appear?" Chances are, if you're reading this book, your answer will be, "I have a weight problem, and I really do need help."

Instead of controlling your weight problem, let's get rid of the problem altogether. God would not have us manage a problem we can eliminate!

If this is the case, welcome to the club. You are not alone—millions of others are in the same boat. You are losing pounds and then putting them back on again. Oftentimes, you are putting more back on than you took off in the first place. As someone once said, "I have lost two hundred pounds, twenty pounds ten times."

If you can relate, this book has been written with you in mind. My prayer is that through your reading of this book and by applying the principles suggested, you will find help. I pray also that your life will be enriched and that you will become reasonably thin.

If you're really serious about controlling your weight problem, let me take you one step farther. Instead of controlling your weight problem, let's get rid of the problem altogether.

God would not have us manage a problem we can eliminate! You may relate to this account of Carolyn.

Carolyn

Carolyn sat on the sofa while I sat in my usual chair. I watched her as she told me of her life and struggles. Something about what she said seemed so familiar.

"This is the only area of my life that I just can't conquer." She continued. "I've tried everything! I've dieted. I've prayed. But nothing ever works; nothing ever lasts! I just can't live this way! I feel as if my life is passing me by. If I could just lose this weight, things would be OK."

In my mind, I could hear the echo of others' voices. Carolyn was saying what they all had said. She broke down, and through her tears I could see not only her pain but the desperate faces of so many others who had come to me for help.

I saw Carolyn as one of an ever growing number of individuals, men and women alike, who struggle with destructive eating behaviors. At that point, I decided not only to treat her in individual therapy, but to take on the problems of overeating and undereating themselves. *Reasonably Thin* is the result of that decision. I used the same information to write this book as I did in dealing with Carolyn and others. They conquered their weight problems, and you can conquer yours too. You've already taken the first step by placing this book in your hands. Let me explain a bit further.

The first step in conquering your weight problem is to acknowledge that you are struggling with your weight. You probably would not be reading this book if that was not the case. You have shown me that you are capable of making decisions that are good for you. By doing this, you have also demonstrated that you have the capacity for success. Those are two more steps. You are already on the journey to becoming reasonably thin.

You are already experiencing success! Pretty exciting, isn't it? Isn't it nice, for just a few moments, to feel relief from the pain and hopelessness of struggling with a weight problem? Let's talk about the pain for just a moment.

God is on your side. He wants you to experience freedom in every area of your life, including this one!

You may have noticed as you were reading that last paragraph that your feelings were at times sad or heavy and, at times, lighter. You may have experienced slight feelings of relief or hope, alternating with fear or desperation or other similar feelings.

Those heavy feelings are the feelings of captivity. You are not alone. Many are captive to them just like you. And these feelings are all common to those in captivity. Those lighter feelings are feelings of hope. But even the feelings of hope are being weighed down by awareness of past failures. So even the feelings of relief have a tinge of hopelessness attached to them. Won't it be wonderful to have feelings of hope without hopelessness attached? *Reasonably Thin* will tell you how to do this. I'll go through it with you as you become reasonably thin, step-by-step. Remember, you have already begun to take important steps! You can take the rest! God is on your side. He wants you to experience freedom in every area of your life, including this one!

Steps to Becoming Reasonably Thin

- Acknowledge that you are struggling with your weight.
- Acknowledge that, by picking up this book, you have demonstrated that you are capable of making decisions that are good for you.
- Acknowledge that, by having made a decision that is good for you, you have demonstrated that you have the capacity for success!

For the LORD hears the needy,
And does not despise His who are prisoners.
—Ps. 69:33 NASB

God is listening to you right now.

Prayer

Father, You know that I'm captive to this struggle with food, with weight. Please use this book to unlock Your truths, and guide me to a life of full freedom in Christ. In the name of Jesus, amen.

2

Choosing
Your Standard

And do not be conformed to this world, but be transformed by the renewing of your mind, that you may prove what is that good and acceptable and perfect will of God.

—Romans 12:2

$\mathcal{A}$ number of futuristic movies have been made depicting a nightmare future where everyone looks and acts just the same. Their looks, thoughts, and behaviors are determined by some external, mechanistic, universal authority. All individuality is gone and the whole of society looks like a fifties suburb gone wrong. That kind of world is not for me. It's not for God either! He made us all different—one societal size does not fit all!

Being reasonably thin means to be the weight that is reasonable for you. This is not about what the media say, what your friends say, or what anyone else says. You must determine what is reasonable for you. You may listen to experts give you excellent recommendations on what your appropriate weight may be. But if you do not determine what being reasonably thin means to you, you are not likely to change. It is important to change from the inside out, not from the outside in!

Every body is different. Your weight will be different from that of others. Some of us will be lighter; some of us will weigh more. Weight is an individual thing. This may sound basic, but it is not as well understood as it should be. As a matter of fact, there are huge industries built on the notion that we all should be more the same and less individualistic. These industries intend to color our thinking and provide us with their mental lenses through which we are to see the world. It is important to be aware of these image-mongers in our environment.

He made us all different—one societal size does not fit all! Being reasonably thin means to be the weight that is reasonable for you.

Do you think that society places pressure on people to be a certain weight? Do magazines, television, motion pictures, the fashion industry, and advertising exert pressure on people to conform to a certain weight? What about diet programs, do they place pressure on people to be a certain weight? What about peer groups and families, can there be pressure from within them to be a certain weight?

The answer to all of these questions is yes. If we give in to the pressure from these areas, we will be subscribing to someone else's definition of what is right for us. It will be someone else's measuring stick, and we will have to adjust when that measuring stick adjusts. But God does not intend for the Christian to be negatively influenced by the world. He does not intend for us to be defined in any way according to what the world says. Instead, He intends the world to be positively influenced by the Christian. Christians will not be able to have this influence if they are looking at this issue from the world's perspective.

Both Christians and non-Christians need to be aware of the influence that is exerted on them by forces outside themselves. This is important because, no matter what the influence is, each individual is responsible for his or her own decisions. Let me use Angie as an example of looking at the weight issue through the wrong lens.

Angie

Angie grew up in a family where the children had to finish everything on their plates before they could leave the table. There were five children, and there was a lot of competition for the food.

"I would always take as much food as I could," Angie said, "because I was afraid that there wouldn't be anything left the second time around. So I always had this big pile of food I had to finish before I could leave the table. I think that's where my weight problem started."

I asked Angie how that affected her weight now.

"I still put too much food on my plate, even when it's just the two of us [Angie and her husband]. And I still feel like I have to finish everything on my plate before I can leave the table."

Angie was overeating because she was still looking at eating through the lens of her family of origin. Even though now there were only two people eating, Angie was still load-ing her plate as if six other people might take her food before she got to it.

Angie had not adjusted her thinking about eating since childhood. That is significant because *our behavior is gener-ated by our thoughts*. Because her thinking about eating had not changed, neither had her eating behavior. That is true with us too. If we look through a lens that says we have to finish everything on our plates, we are far more likely to do just that.

Angie's eating behavior was also being driven, in large part, by her feelings. She overloaded her plate because she was afraid that there would not be enough food left for her. She was looking through a lens distorted by feelings—in this case fear. She did not see the food as it actually was—ample and available. She saw it as at risk and fleeting. Again, Angie acted on the bias of the lens rather than on what was actually true.

K nowing the truth is not enough. Once we know the truth, the next step is to apply the principle of faith.

Once Angie learned to adjust her lens, she was on the way to being reasonably thin. How about you? Are you still look-ing at this issue through someone else's lens? Are you look-ing through a lens biased by the past or unresolved issues? By the time you have finished *Reasonably Thin*, you will have had the opportunity to explore and change those lenses. I will show you, as I did Angie, exactly how to adjust the lenses through which you see yourself and your world.

Together, we will take those lens adjustments on, one by one, step-by-step! Let me give you a glimpse of how it is done.

Adjusting our lenses is done by holding everything that we think up to what the Bible says, and changing our thinking to reflect the biblical perspective. In short we will adjust our lenses by telling the truth. It is more than just taking in information. We'll be renewing our minds. By that I mean we will be continually growing in knowing the truth, and in being able to recognize what is not true in areas related to weight issues. As we do that, our thinking will begin to conform to the truth. I will provide you with the biblical perspective throughout this book.

Knowing the truth is not enough. Once we know the truth, the next step is to apply the principle of faith: We will take the truths we learn from God about our weight issues and apply those truths to our lives by acting on them. God will honor these actions because they are what He wants for our lives. For the non-Christian, these truths may be applied in their own strength. For the Christian, God will actually empower your actions with His strength. Let me explain: When someone becomes a Christian, the Holy Spirit comes to live within that person. When the Christian turns to God and relies on His strength to do His will in the Christian's life, the indwelling Holy Spirit provides the strength for the task. We are exercising our faith in God by acting on the truths He gives us. When we do that, He promises to bless us in what we are doing. In this book I will show you how to apply God's truths to your life.

In the long run, we are talking about obedience. We are talking about doing what is right for us and best for us. It means obeying God in this area and not living by feelings or by any perspective other than God's. I will be talking to you about obedience and what that looks like in practicality.

The final thing we will learn how to do is to endure. I will show you how to keep on applying what you have already learned about your weight issues as you continue to learn more. *Reasonably Thin* will continue to take you through the entire process, step-by-step!

Steps to Becoming Reasonably Thin

- Acknowledge that there are outside influences trying to convince you what your weight should be.
- Acknowledge that these influences can provide you with lenses through which you may look at your weight issues.
- Determine that the only lens through which you will look at your weight issues will be the Bible—the truth.

Prayer

Father, unlock my mind and show me where I have any tendencies to conform to the world's notion of what my weight should be. Please help me develop the biblical lens through which to see this issue. Please use this book to guide me to the reasonable weight for me, according to You. May I put on Your Word as I would put on corrective glasses, showing me with clarity Your truth about this issue in my life. In the name of Jesus, amen.

3

Freeing Yourself from the Tyranny of Food

Therefore we also, since we are surrounded by so great a cloud of witnesses, let us lay aside every weight, and the sin which so easily ensnares us, and let us run with endurance the race that is set before us, looking unto Jesus.
—Hebrews 12:1–2

Laying Aside Every Weight

As I dealt with individuals who were struggling with weight issues, I began to notice that they had a number of similar tendencies, which I think of as encumbrances. I found that if they could eliminate or adjust those tendencies that they had in common, they could conquer their weight problem. By allowing these encumbrances to affect our thinking, feeling, and behavior, we may subject ourselves to their captivity, holding ourselves back from being all that God would have us be.

Our thinking is what drives our feelings and our behavior. If our thinking is flawed, our feelings will also be flawed. If our thinking and feelings are flawed, our behavior will inevitably be flawed. Let me give you an example.

Thinking that you must be perfect in the area of weight will lead to disappointment and feelings of failure. If you tend to eat to comfort yourself during emotional distress, you are then likely to overeat. If you tend to punish yourself for not being perfect, you might either starve yourself or overeat. Here is another example.

> *As I dealt with individuals who were struggling with weight issues, I began to notice that they had a number of similar tendencies, which I think of as encumbrances. I found that if they could eliminate or adjust those tendencies that they had in common, they could conquer their weight problem.*

If you think passively, as if your weight problem is happening *to you,* you will likely feel like a victim. You will feel helpless and hopeless, feelings that may lead to depression. If you eat to comfort yourself, you may overeat in response to feeling hopeless. If you think passively, you are not likely to see your own power to correct the situation and that may lead to resigning yourself to failure.

Thinking passively, thinking perfectionistically, expecting the worst, focusing on the negative, thinking in extremes, and many other unfortunate ways of thinking tend to be common among those who struggle with weight. Usually no one of us has all of these tendencies, but when we are struggling with a weight issue, we often have a number of them. You will have the opportunity to encounter and deal with your tendencies as we go through the book together.

You might find it interesting that the term *weight* in our opening verse means "encumbrance, excess weight, weight that hinders the effectiveness of the runner in the race." One may think of it as a runner trying to run a race while wearing boots made of lead. It would be the weight that the athlete works to get rid of during training for the upcoming race. I think of it as anything holding us back, including excessive concerns about weight. Dealing with extra weight in our Christian lives takes up our time, robs us of our joy, and affects our effectiveness.

Applying this definition to your own life, would you agree that chronic concern with your weight is an encumbrance? Is it something that is holding you back from being *all* that you can be in Jesus Christ? Is it holding you back from experiencing *all* of the freedom that belongs to you in Jesus Christ? Do you live your life encumbered with worry about weight, fear of rejection, and all of the other concerns that are connected to overeating or undereating? An encumbrance inhibits us and keeps us from our highest and best.

The apostle Paul, one of the writers of the New Testament, said this about encumbrances: We are to "lay them aside." By an act of our will, we are to lay aside every encumbrance, and that includes any and all bondage related to food.

For our purposes, the concept of encumbrance will include any thoughts or behaviors that would in any way inhibit our spiritual, emotional, or psychological growth and that would keep us from being all that God would have us be. We will look, in particular, at those encumbering thoughts, feelings, and behaviors related to overeating, undereating, and more.

Would you agree that excessive concern with your weight is an encumbrance? Does it hold you back from being all that you could be in Him, all that you could be in general? If you are a Christian, this does not mean that God is not working in your life. It just means that there is one area that is not all that it could be. If you agree that this chronic and excessive concern with weight is an encumbrance, then does this chronic and excessive concern with weight have to go? Are you willing to consider how you may do that? If you answered those questions with a yes, then once again, you have taken even more steps on the journey to becoming reasonably thin! Now, let's listen to Beth to get a glimpse of some of those encumbrances I've been talking about.

Beth

When Beth came to me for treatment she was seriously depressed.

"I've been suffering from being overweight since I was twenty-eight," she said. "It's almost destroyed my life. I feel like such a failure."

I asked what she meant when she said that being overweight had almost destroyed her life.

"When we first got married I was in perfect shape, so life was great. My husband and I were very active. We were both attending a Christian college and were extremely social. Then the children began to arrive one by one, and things started to change."

I asked what had changed.

"Well, all of a sudden he was at work, and I was at home with the children. I'd put on weight with each of the children, and it just kept accumulating. Eventually, I just gave up."

Let's take a look at some of the things Beth was saying.

Most of them are similar to what others who struggle with weight have said. You might even recognize some of your own thoughts in here.

Beth said, "I was in perfect shape, so life was great." That statement suggested to me that Beth based too much of her perception of how well she was doing in life on her weight. It also suggested to me that Beth tended toward perfectionism. This statement told me that she was likely to set her standards too high and base her success on her weight alone. This type of thinking leads to inevitable failure, because no one on this earth is perfect, and basing our entire self-esteem on our weight is asking our weight to bear more than it actually can.

Beth said, "I've been suffering from being overweight" and "It's [the weight has] almost destroyed my life." She also said, "The weight just kept accumulating." These statements suggested that Beth tended to see things as happening *to her*, instead of her actively *causing things to happen*. People who think passively are more likely than not to see themselves as victims, as Beth did. That type of thinking causes feelings of helplessness and hopelessness. Those who think this way feel that they have no control over the situation. This type of thinking was just another wall in Beth's self-imposed prison of seeming helplessness.

When people think things are helpless, they tend to resign themselves to their circumstances. You can see that in Beth's statements: "I feel like such a failure." "Eventually, I just gave up." The cycle is complete. The wrong thinking led to wrong feeling, which led to wrong behavior. This type of thinking, feeling, and behavior is what I consider an encumbrance, with which we hold ourselves back from being all that God would have us be.

The truth was that even though Beth's concern with weight tended to dominate her thoughts and feelings, and even though she saw herself as defeated, she was not. The only thing she was willing to see was defeat. A part of the change that she had to bring about in her own thinking was that she had to be willing to see her successes and to capitalize on them. She had to understand the nature of passive thinking, then to learn and determine to think actively. I showed Beth how to emerge successfully from the captivity of these encumbrances; I will do the same with you.

Chemical changes can occur with childbirth, or with growing older, and those changes can affect weight. Beth assumed that that was the source of her weight problem. My suggestion to Beth was that she apply the principles of *Reasonably Thin*, and we would deal with anything that remained. Beth found that when she applied the principles of *Reasonably Thin*, both her weight and her excessive concerns with food began to fall off. She no longer struggles with weight.

Apparently, the chemical changes that may have occurred with having children were not the reason for Beth's weight gain. But her assumption that the chemical changes were the cause contributed to her sense of helplessness. All of this wrong thinking and the results of it weighed Beth down Once she faced every thought and conformed it to the truth, she began to lay aside the excess weights of wrong thinking, wrong feeling, and wrong behavior and Beth began for the first time to run the race unencumbered.

Beth found the answers she was looking for by opening up her thoughts, feelings, and behavior to evaluation. Are you willing to look at your own thoughts, feelings, and behavior? Then keep reading, and I will show you how it is done. Remember—you can only lay aside the encumbrances you are willing to see.

Steps to Becoming Reasonably Thin

- Acknowledge that your chronic and excessive concern with weight is an encumbrance.
- Acknowledge that this encumbrance is holding you back from being all that you can be in Christ.
- Acknowledge that this encumbrance must go!
- Have a willingness to obey God's mandate to lay aside this encumbrance!

Prayer

Father, I open my mind and my feelings to You. Please, throughout the course of this book, show me what needs changing and how to change. I want to be all that You want me to be. In the name of Jesus, amen.

4

Moving from Passive
to Active Thinking

*Whoever digs a pit will fall into it,
And he who rolls a stone will have it roll back on
him.*

—Proverbs 26:27

$\mathcal{S}$ome counselors base their
theory on Maslow, Freud, or Rogers. Not me. Like any good
counselor raised in America in the fifties, I base my theoretical orientation on Wyle E. Coyote and the Roadrunner, cartoon characters by Chuck Jones. The theory is very simple.
If you place an anvil high atop a fragile ledge and you stand
underneath it, the anvil will fall on you. If you then refuse to
acknowledge that you were the one who caused the problem
by putting the anvil there, you will do it again, and it will fall
on you again. Further, if you continue with this approach,
you will never solve the original problem!

When I was a kid, I used to watch Wyle E. Coyote repeatedly set up some ingenious plan to capture his uncatchable nemesis, Roadrunner. Each time he did, the plan turned around and snared Wyle E. instead. I kept having conversations with the Wyle E. Coyote: "No, don't do that! That anvil is going to land on you, not on Roadrunner!" and "Don't you see that if you strap yourself to that rocket, you'll blow up with it?" But alas! He never listened to me. As a result, zillions of his coyote bucks went for ACME gadgets, none of which caught the Roadrunner. And Wyle E., in addition to never capturing the Roadrunner, never got a clue!

It is one thing to say, "I suffer from being overweight or underweight." It is another thing to say, "I cause myself to suffer by overeating or undereating."

I learned in this process that talking to cartoon characters was not necessarily productive for them, but it certainly was for me. These conversations were, in likelihood, the early stages of my development as a counselor. After all, counseling frequently deals with Coyote-and Roadrunner-type antics.

Like Wyle E. Coyote, many who struggle with weight issues accidentally sabotage themselves. They set themselves up for failure by suggesting that they are not the cause of their weight problem. Because of that, they are always developing strategies that don't address the real problem.

It is one thing to say, "I *suffer from* being overweight or underweight." It is another thing to say, "I *cause myself to suffer* by overeating or undereating." To say the first is to assume a victim stance and to encourage a sense of helplessness. To say the second is to assume responsibility, and in that there is hope. When you ou take responsibility you can generate change.

It will be important for you to accept responsibility for your weight problem to the degree that you cause it. To that same degree, it will be important for you to learn to say, "I cause myself to suffer by overeating or undereating" instead of saying, "I suffer from being over- or underweight."

I mentioned in the previous chapter that I saw similarities among those who struggle with weight issues that I consider to be encumbrances. Here is one of the big ones: thinking passively rather than thinking actively. Here is the difference: In passive thinking, you think that things are happening to you. In active thinking, you think that you are causing things to happen. If you move from passive thinking to active thinking, becoming reasonably thin is within reach! Ken would be an excellent example here.

Ken

When Ken walked into the office, his presence changed the environment. He had an air about him. He seemed so in charge and intelligent. As an attorney, I'm sure he made quite an impact on a jury. But Ken had a problem.

Ever since becoming a partner in a law firm, Ken had been putting on weight. I asked him about the weight gain, and this is the account he gave me.

"When I started with the firm I felt successful. The work was nonstop, but as I began to move up the ladder, things became more social. There were lunches with clients, dinners with the partners, late-night dinners, ordering in at all hours. The food just kept coming, and the weight just kept building up. Now, I'm not feeling quite so successful."

I asked if we could revisit one of those comments.

Lawyers love to revisit things! I asked him what he meant by "the weight just kept building up."

He said, "I meant that the weight just kept piling on."

"Are you saying that the food actually attacked you?" I asked. "Do you mean 'piling on,' like in football, where all the guys from one team jump on the one guy from the other team?" Fortunately, Ken understood my humor and accepted my point. I explained to Ken that he was thinking passively. It was as if the food were somehow attaching itself to him, without any encouragement on his part.

"This is one of the major errors in thinking associated with weight problems," I said. "When we think passively, we don't take responsibility for our behavior. Conquering weight problems requires taking responsibility for our thoughts and behaviors."

When Ken dissected his comment that "the weight just kept building up," he found a great deal of personal responsibility inside. I had him rephrase his comment in a way that demonstrated that he was actually taking action, instead of being passive. When he put the comment in the active mode, it came out in these statements: "I began to eat more. I began to exercise less. I began to eat foods that were higher in fat content. I began to eat late at night. I began to eat in a hurry. I began to eat under pressure. I began to eat when I wasn't hungry. I began to eat to please others. I began to eat when I didn't want to." Active thinking removed the fog and confusion from the issue of his weight gain. It actually revealed the mechanics of how he gained his weight. That is important because we will not fix what we will not, or cannot, see!

In changing his thinking from passive to active thinking, Ken began to deal honestly with his weight problem. It was a very important step in his successful journey to becoming reasonably thin. Are you willing to dissect your thoughts and make those same changes? Look at the difference between active and passive thinking.

———

Remember how Ken kept saying that the weight just kept piling on? That is passive thinking. Passive thinking suggests that your weight problem is something passively happening to you and that you are not responsible. Remember when Ken said that he had begun to eat more? That was Ken switching to active thinking. Active thinking acknowledges that you are actively causing your weight problem with your own thinking and behavior.

> *Hope is found in being able to access God's power in dealing with our weight issues.*

Passive thinking encouraged Ken's sense of hopelessness. It will do the same to you if you subscribe to it. If you think your weight problem is just happening to you, you will think it is out of your control. That leads to your thinking that you are helpless to change it. Active thinking, on the other hand, encouraged Ken's sense of hope. If you are able to choose defeat in your eating behavior you are also demonstrating that you have the capacity to choose victory in your eating behavior.

Passive thinking demonstrates your willingness to be a victim. With it, you may destroy your self-esteem. Passive thinking does not represent Christlikeness. Active thinking demonstrates your willingness to be a responsible individual. With it, you will build your self-esteem. Active thinking does represent Christlikeness. Ken got the point. You will,

too, as you continue to read through and work through
Reasonably Thin.

Assignment:

Purchase a journal. Begin to record your thoughts and
statements that you think are passive. Then change them to
active statements, and write that change in your journal.
Make note, too, of your active statements, in which you take
responsibility for your thoughts and behavior. Allow yourself
to feel good about having caught the passive statements, and
having changed them to active statements. This is a very
important accomplishment!

Examples:

Passive: This weight problem is just destroying me.
Active: I'm destroying myself by overeating or undereating.
You will know you are ready to quit journaling on this
topic when there are no more passive entries.

Hope is found in being able to access God's power in dealing with our weight issues. If we think passively we will not
access His power completely. We may ask God to change our
environment or reduce temptation. But to fully access God's
power in this area requires something else: It is only when
we acknowledge our part in our weight problem that we can
turn to Him to empower us to do what is right. If we think
passively, we will see no need to have God empower us. If
we think actively, we will.

For the Christian there is always hope. But when we think
passively, we cause delay in our hopes being fulfilled. That
causes heartache and pain. As Christians, we must remember
that a life of victory is our birthright. It is time to think actively
and grab on to hope, riding it to its fulfillment. You can do it!
Stay on the road to becoming reasonably thin! Endure!

For the non-Christian, passive thinking robs you of success that you may accomplish in your own power. Learning to think actively will give you back your self-control.

Steps to Becoming Reasonably Thin

- Recognize that there are two different types of thinking that affect your weight struggle: active thinking and passive thinking.
- Acknowledge that passive thinking leads to a sense of helplessness and a sense of loss of control.
- Acknowledge that active thinking builds self-esteem.
- Acknowledge that you have control over your weight issues.
- Recognize that thinking actively or thinking passively is a choice.
- Be willing to learn to think actively.
- Choose to think actively.
- Refuse to think passively!

Hope deferred makes the heart sick,
But when the desire comes, it is a tree of life.
—Proverbs 13:12

Prayer

Father, I open up to You my longings to conquer this weight problem. I trust You to lead me to fulfilling these longings. Point out to me any passive thinking, any way that I think of this problem as happening to me. I know that passive thinking will hold the fulfillment of my hopes at bay. Strengthen me to think actively, taking responsibility for my weight problem, so that in Your strength I may take responsibility for my success. In the name of Jesus, amen.

5

Choosing the Right Goal

He is a double-minded man, unstable in all his ways.

—James 1:8

While shopping I ran across a very peculiar picture with colors and wavy lines that to me seemed incomprehensible. The big sign by the picture said "Find the shark in the picture!" And I did in about a half hour when my eyes finally crossed in that way parents say will last forever if you ever do it! The trick was to not look for the shark but to back off, blur your vision a bit, and the shark would show up. And he did! The whole picture was all about perspective. That is how it is with weight issues too.

Our perspective is critical. If we focus on our weight, we will encourage obsessing on the problem at the expense of the solution. If we focus on losing weight in order to glorify God, we have added an unnecessary and detrimental step to the process. The focus is back on the problem and not the solution.

If we focus on weight management, we simply learn to keep the problem alive. God would not have us manage this problem. He would have us not have the problem at all! Why manage what we can eliminate?

> *If we focus on weight management, we simply learn to keep the problem alive. God would not have us manage this problem. He would have us not have the problem at all!*

Let's consider the New Testament Scripture that is quoted at the beginning of this chapter. In its context (vv. 5–8) James was encouraging Christians who desire wisdom to ask God for that wisdom and stating that God will provide it. But he wrote that we should ask without doubting, because vacillating between doubting and believing causes us to be unstable in our life and in our requests we make of God. This instability also occurs when we vacillate between two different thoughts, and in the case of weight struggles, between two different goals.

Let's say we determine to lose weight in order to please our spouse, and we also decide to lose weight to improve our self-esteem. We do have one goal—to lose weight—although our interests will be divided as to our purposes, which are to improve self-esteem and to please our spouse. That alone places our success in jeopardy. But the problem here is that we will also have other goals in life. We may have additional goals such as setting a certain amount of money aside for retirement or succeeding in a career. Now we have three goals. Our energy will be divided among the three, and we will become unstable in accomplishing them.

Let's define a goal as being the overall attainment. It is what you want to achieve as the end result of all you do. The most important thing about a goal is to have only one. The words of Jesus in Matthew 22:37 demonstrate an example of single-mindedness: "You shall love the LORD your God with all your heart, with all your soul, and with all your mind." Notice the word *all* and how it is repeated in the verse. We are to love the Lord with our entire being. And, whatever our goal will be, it must include the focus of loving God in this all-encompassing way. We must single-mindedly focus on one well-determined goal. To do otherwise is to divide our attentions and dilute our focus. Then we become double-minded and unstable on the point.

> *Our goal should be to glorify God in this area as we are to do in all areas of our lives.*

We must not attempt to lose weight to please our husbands or wives, to feel better, to fit into those new clothes, to improve our self-esteem, to look better, or to be healthier, because those reasons are too narrow in their focus. This may be what you want to do in regard to losing weight, but that is only one area of your life. As Christians, we need to look at the whole truth of our lives and determine a goal that covers every action.

So, what should be our goal? What goal is broad enough to pertain to every area of our lives but specific enough to accomplish all of the things that we want to accomplish? What goal, if achieved, will also resolve our weight issues? It is the answer to this question: What is the goal of the Christian life? Let's take it straight from the Bible. Look at what the apostle Paul tells us on this point in 1 Corinthians 10:31: "Therefore, whether you eat or drink, or whatever you do, do all to the glory of God."

Our goal should be to glorify God in this area as we are to do in all areas of our lives. Our goal should not be to lose weight or to manage our weight problem. Again, our goal should be to glorify God. All else will fall into place after that. This will be an essential shift in our thinking as we continue along this journey. Let's take a look at the goal of someone who came to me for treatment.

Jean

I asked Jean what she wanted out of therapy.

"I want to lose twenty pounds," she said. "I know I would feel so much better about myself if I could just lose this weight!" The look on her face was a strained mixture of doubt and hope—I could almost feel it.

"What is the doubt that I see on your face?" I asked her.

As she thought about the question, the look on her face turned to grief. Tears welled up in her eyes and began to overflow as she tried to speak.

"It feels like a heavy weight pulling me under. I want to believe that I can do this, but I'm beginning to feel it's impossible. I'm a Christian, and I know I shouldn't feel this way."

"And where did the hope that I saw in your face come from?" I explored further.

"I want to do this," Jean said. "I want so badly to accomplish this goal. I just don't know why I can't get it done. I feel like such a failure."

Exercise

Let's tie what we have learned about passive thinking in to what we are learning now. See if you can identify the passive statement in what Jean said. Remember, it will be a statement that suggests that something is happening to her, without her being responsible. You may write it on the line below if you would like.

_____

This was her passive statement: "It feels like a heavy weight pulling me under."

Write the statement on the line below, but write it in the active mode.

_____

Here is one way to state it in the active mode: "Because of the way I'm eating, I feel like I'm pulling myself under."

Remember, it is important to put your thinking into active mode, because that encourages you to take responsibility for your thinking and behavior. When you take responsibility for your thinking and behavior, you then have the power to change it!

Read the account of Jean again. What was her stated goal? It was to lose twenty pounds. Let's take a look at what was wrong with her goal.

Jean's goal was too narrow. Her goal applied to only one area of her life—her weight. This would force her to have other goals for other areas, and her attention would be divided. She would then have less energy to invest in the area of weight. This would lead to being double-minded and unstable on the issue. Do you tend to feel unstable in the area of your weight? It may be because you have the wrong goal.

Again, Jean's goal was to lose twenty pounds. Her goal focused on her weight! Her goal actually focused on the problem! Focusing on the problem can lead to obsessing on the problem. In this case, focusing on losing weight had Jean focusing on food! Focusing on food encourages weight problems! The paradox of the entire weight management industry is that it encourages those who want to lose weight to focus on the issue of food!

Do you tend to obsess on food? Your goal related to weight control may be part of the problem. Having the goal of glorifying God in all things removes you from the emotional pull of weight management. That allows you to deal with the problem from a more objective position.

> *The paradox of the entire weight management industry is that it encourages those who want to lose weight to focus on the issue of food!*

Her focus on food was further intensified by the attachment of a specific number. Jean wanted to lose twenty pounds. Not only was she focusing on the problem, she was intensely focused to the point of knowing exactly how much weight she should lose. The more specific her goal was in this area, the more anxiety would be attached to it. She would end up eating just to calm the anxiety. Do you tend to experience high anxiety when you try to manage your weight? You may be too intensely focused on it. Jean was. With her anxiety, Jean was driving herself to eat destructively.

Let me just add one more thing that Jean was doing. She was counting calories. That encouraged her involvement and obsession with food to be even more intensified! Jean was driven in the area of weight management—it consumed her; it controlled her. God would have led her in a different direction, because in the areas in which people are driven, they cannot be led.

Once her focus had shifted away from weight and weight management, Jean was freed from substantial anxiety. She was then more at ease and well on the path to becoming reasonably thin.

If we eat in a way that brings glory to God, we won't have a weight problem. If we spend in a way that brings glory to God, we won't have a spending problem. If we drive . . . if we love . . . if we live in a way that brings glory to God, our problems will not be self-inflicted. Becoming reasonably thin will be the by-product of glorifying God in the area of our weight issues.

Steps to Becoming Reasonably Thin

- Have one singular goal in your life: to glorify God in all things!
- Determine not to manage your weight problem. Instead, allow it to be eliminated by having and acting on the right goal.

Prayer

Father, I'm changing the way I think now. Please help me hold in my mind securely that my goal is to glorify You in all I do. That includes the area of weight. Please empower me to eliminate what You would not have me manage. And lead me on. In the name of Jesus, amen.

6

Focusing on
the Right Things

*Let us run with endurance the race that is set
before us, looking unto Jesus.*
—Hebrews 12:1–2

W hat do you think would hap-
pen if a runner in a race concentrated on avoiding the other
runners or avoiding losing? A substantial amount of their
focus would be behind them or on what they are afraid of,
and that could cost them the race. The best runners in the
race never look back. They focus on what is in front of them,
because looking back or fearing defeat takes some of the
runner's energy, time, balance, and concentration. The best
runners are not willing to sacrifice any of those four. That is
part of what makes them winners. Their strategy is not built
on avoidance; it is built on reaching the end of the race first.

Have you ever tried so hard not to do something that you
ended up doing it anyway? I have done that with typing. I

will notice that I am typing fast. Then, I start thinking about how I do not want to make a mistake. The next thing I know, I have made a mistake in typing!

Why is it that when we try so hard not to do something we often do it anyway? It's because we are focusing our thoughts—and because of that, our energies—on that very thing we are trying to avoid. That produces the likelihood that we will do the very thing we are trying not to do.

There are times and places when avoidance is a good idea and it works well. When using power tools or when cooking, it is important to plan to cook and work in safe ways. But when those safety measures are in place there is no need to focus on the possible dangers.

When it comes to weight issues, plans for avoidance can become a part of the problem. Let me use Kathleen's story about her struggle with food to show you why this happens and what you can do about it.

Kathleen

In an attempt to curb her eating behavior and to cut down on her thinking about food, Kathleen devised a strategy, a plan of avoidance. Let's see how it worked.

"When I go to the mall, I have to avoid the food areas,." Kathleen said. "I deliberately walk across to the other side of the mall when I know the cookie place is just a few stores in front of me. Or I look the other way as I go by the food court."

"So, do you enjoy going to the mall?" I asked, anticipating that she would say she did not enjoy it.

"Are you kidding?" she shot back at me. "I'm a nervous wreck, trying to avoid all of those places. Ever since I've been doing that, I've become even more aware of how many food places there are in the mall. I even have to avoid places inside the department stores! I'll bet I can tell you where every food place is inside the mall!"

Why was it that Kathleen's plan of avoiding food seemed to cause her to be even more preoccupied with it? It had to do with Kathleen's focus. Her focus was on the wrong thing.

I had Kathleen actually draw a quick sketch for me of the mall, and she really could tell me where most of the food areas were! She had just demonstrated what happens when we try to avoid food. By trying to avoid food, we actually become more focused on it!

> *When it comes to weight issues, plans for avoidance can become a part of the problem.*

Kathleen thought she was focusing on the solution but, in fact, she was focusing on the problem. Here is what happened. Kathleen was emotionally invested in her plan to avoid food. Added to that, she had an expectation attached to her plan of avoiding food. She expected to avoid food. That expectation created anxiety around the issue of food. Because of this expectation, if she was successful in the plan, she would feel good. If she failed in the plan, she would feel badly. If she did fail, her feeling badly would likely encourage her destructive eating.

This was part of the eating problem or what I will call destructive eating behavior. Focusing on avoiding food had Kathleen thinking indirectly about food. That created an indirect obsession with food. The more places she avoided, the more her plan required her to think about food. The more she carried out her plan, the more she thought about food, and the less successful she felt. She created more anxiety by focusing on avoiding food.

Eventually Kathleen succumbed to her unintentionally self-inflicted obsession with food and ate when she had not planned to. She ate, in fact, when she had planned not to eat. Then she felt extremely bad because her plan had failed. That was accompanied by more feelings of anxiety over her failure. Since Kathleen had a history of eating to relieve anxiety, she overate and caused her weight problem to grow even worse! Focusing on the problem makes the problem worse!

> *You can't be thinking about food when your thoughts are somewhere else.*

There was something else about Kathleen's focus that caused her difficulty. It may cause you difficulty, if you do the same. Her focus was on the negative. Her plan was built around what she didn't want to do, rather than on what she wanted to do. Instead of having excitement over doing what she wanted to do, she experienced the anxiety associated with guarding against failure. Without knowing it, Kathleen had set herself up for failure. This is what can happen when we concentrate so much on not doing a certain thing. We may lead ourselves into doing that very thing.

When Kathleen was focusing on avoiding food, she was not able to focus on anything else. Why did that happen? Because you cannot think two thoughts at the exact same time, although you can go back and forth between thoughts. That tells us something. Focusing on one thing can only be done at the expense of focusing on another.

So, why is that important when it comes to dealing with food? If you are excessively focused on food, it's at the expense of other interests in your life. Also, if you are busy focusing on the problem, you cannot at the same time focus on the solution. And, here is the other side of that same coin: You can't be thinking about food when your thoughts are somewhere else.

I did with Kathleen what I have done with so many others. I recommended that she not concentrate so much on food. I suggested she do that by simply learning to enjoy other things in life, without food attached. It was not only a great help to her in overcoming her weight problem, but she also learned to enjoy life far more abundantly! For Kathleen, becoming reasonably thin was a way of finding new life in many more areas than just her weight.

Here are some of the reminders and recommendations I gave to Kathleen. Now they are for you, too, on your journey toward becoming reasonably thin.

Steps to Becoming Reasonably Thin

- Don't plan to avoid food.
- Instead, make a reasonable plan for when you will eat, and stick to that plan.
- Plan to do other things that are not related to food.
- Develop an interest in other things that don't involve food.
- By learning to do other things that don't involve food, you will allow yourself to lose interest in food as an activity.
- If you do that, you will allow food to resume its proper place, as a matter of sustenance, rather than as an activity or entertainment.

Prayer

Father, open my eyes and show me more of what there is to living in Christ. Release in me a spirit of adventure, in being open to go where You would lead me. Let me look through Your eyes, in every situation, so that I will develop deeper and more interests in life on Your behalf. Take me forward, Father. In the name of Jesus, amen.

7

Choosing the Right Belief

Finally, brethren, whatever things are true, whatever things are noble, whatever things are just, whatever things are pure, whatever things are lovely, whatever things are of good report, if there is any virtue and if there is anything praiseworthy—meditate on these things.
—Philippians 4:8

I remember traveling across the country with my family when I was a little girl. I remember, too, staying in motels and swimming in the pools. On more than one occasion, I had this same experience. I would dive off the diving board into what I had been told by the motel management would be wonderful, warm water. Imagine my surprise when, on entering the water, I encountered the startling truth—it was ice cold! Sometimes the truth sets you free, and sometimes it makes you feel like a Popsicle!

We act on what we believe. That is why it is important for us to know, not only what we believe, but that what we believe is the truth. For those of us who are Christians, we

43

are to live and think according to the truth. Unfortunately, that is not always what happens. Knowing and believing the truth are not automatic. We have to come to know it then choose to believe it.

Here is an example of what I mean. Many Christians who struggle with weight issues feel helpless about their struggle. But are they in fact helpless? When someone is a Christian, they have Christ living within, by the power of His Holy Spirit. God promises that He will provide all that we ever need to live in a way that honors Him. In 2 Peter 1:2–3, Peter said, "Grace and peace be multiplied to you in the knowledge of God and of Jesus our Lord, as His divine power has given to us all things that pertain to life and godliness, through the knowledge of Him who called us."

We can see from this verse that whatever we need to live in a way that honors God we have already been given in Christ. If our goal is to honor God in the area of our eating, then what we need to accomplish that is already ours. But how do we access what we have been given?

Christians have immediate access to God our Father through Jesus Christ who indwells the Christian. We call this "new birth," where Christ comes into our lives and gives us spiritual life. We access what we need through prayer and faith. In prayer we talk with God about what we are experiencing and request His wisdom and power to deal with various situations. He provides that wisdom through the Bible and through the wise counsel of others. Because we are asking for His wisdom and power to do what will honor Him, He will provide it. When we act on the wise counsel He has provided, we are acting in faith. That is what living by faith is—acting on what God says because you believe Him.

How does that look when it comes to your weight struggle? In this book you will find biblical principles that, if applied in faith, will set you free from the bondage of food and of weight management. Your responsibility is to read the material, praying that God will reveal His truths to you. Then ask God to provide you with the power to follow the guidelines consistently and thoroughly. He will provide the power as you do what the principles and exercises suggest. By doing this you are working in a cooperative way with God. You are living by faith, and that honors God.

> *If we, as Christians, believe that we are helpless, it is because we have chosen that belief.*

As you can see, Christians are anything but helpless. It is with the mistaken perception that they are helpless that they inadvertently hold themselves back. The problem with Christians is that they ask God for the power to accomplish their task, and then they wait for Him to do the work. That is not how it works. He provides the power. We do the work.

What is the non-Christian to do? A great deal can be accomplished in the power of any individual. The Bible refers to that as the power of the flesh. It is possible, in the flesh, to do all that I propose in the way of principles and exercises in this book, except this one thing: Paul wrote to the Roman Christians, in Romans 8:8, in the New Testament, "So then, those who are in the flesh cannot please God."

I add this here because, while non-Christians can use this book to relieve themselves of the struggle with weight, my hope for them is more than that. It is one thing to rid ourselves of our struggles with weight. It is another thing to please God. That requires the new life I spoke of earlier.

Here is Paul again in Romans 8:9: "But you are not in the flesh but in the Spirit, if indeed the Spirit of God dwells in you. Now if anyone does not have the Spirit of Christ, he is not His."

I know this verse can be alarming to non-Christians. But you have the choice of gaining spiritual life, if you choose. At the back of the book I will describe to you how you can become a Christian. The choice is yours. You may rid yourself of your struggle with weight. And if you want to move beyond that to the extraordinary spiritual life of the Christian, you may do that too. Now, let me say a few more things to the Christians reading this book.

If we, as Christians, believe that we are helpless, it is because we have chosen that belief. Both Christians and non-Christians can choose to believe erroneously. Since we act on our beliefs, choosing to believe we are helpless will lead to our living helplessly, even though we are not helpless. At that point, that belief is not only fraudulent, but to the degree that we act on that belief, our lives are fraudulent. False beliefs are encumbrances we choose that hold us back from being all that we can be in Christ. They are the lead boots that we choose to wear while running in the race of life.

Here are just a few false beliefs that thrive among those who struggle with their weight. One is the false belief that our weight problems, either the cause or the cure, are dependent on someone else. That leads to the false belief that the doctor or weight specialist should fix us. Acting on such a belief is part of what keeps us hooked on weight-loss programs and weight management programs. These beliefs imply that our weight problems exist because someone close to us sabotages us or because society pushes food upon us constantly. These false beliefs give us false justification to feel that our weight issues are out of our control.

Also, there is the false belief that the only change we need is in how we *eat*, rather than how we *think*. But if our thinking does not change, the struggle will live on. This false belief is a part of what allows us to depend on what others think and on others to tell us how to eat. We remain dependent on those other people or systems because we have not learned to change our thinking. We need to know the mechanics of how to do that ourselves. This book will provide you with the tools to do just that.

Another false belief is that we should be one perfect weight. We will discuss perfectionistic thinking later in this book. To reach that perfection there is the false belief that there is some magic pill that will solve all weight problems. Let's take a look at Beth, who subscribed to that false belief.

Beth

Beth told me that she had tried to take the weight off many times. "I used diet pills for years," she said. "I've spent thousands of dollars on liposuction and, for a matter of months, things are fine. Then the weight comes back."

Initially, when Beth came to me for treatment, she was looking for medication to relieve her depression. While I did refer her for an evaluation for medications for depression, I knew that medications were not going to solve her weight problem. Having heard her story, I was not surprised that Beth would pursue a chemical solution to the problem.

If you look back over her statements, you may be able to see the indicators in what Beth said that suggest she might lean toward a "quick fix." Beth made these statements in regard to weight reduction: "I used diet pills for years" and "I've spent thousands of dollars on liposuction."

Not only was there the presence of statements that indicate Beth had tried "shortcuts" as a solution to her problem, there was an absence of statements regarding any other types of attempts to solve the problem. With Beth, the encumbrance that held her back from being all that she could be was her holding on to a false belief.

Beth invested her time in the search for the magic pill or the magic treatment. The only problem with that is that there is no magic pill and there is no magic treatment. That search was endless and futile. The search for the magic pill or the magic treatment, in itself, can result in depression and despair. That depression and despair may become the catalyst for harmful eating patterns.

If Beth had taken a strictly chemical approach to her problem, she would likely have failed to relieve herself of it and created only more problems in the process. Instead, she decided to let go of her false beliefs and give up her futile search for shortcuts. When she did, she became responsible for her own destructive eating behavior and began to change it. By making these changes and following the principles in this book, Beth became, and has remained, reasonably thin. How about you? Are you ready to give up your false beliefs? Those who are reasonably thin hold no false beliefs related to food!

Steps to Becoming Reasonably Thin

- Stop looking for something outside yourself to resolve your destructive eating.
- Keep on reading and learn how to look to Christ within.
- Remember: By investing your energy in looking for the wrong approach you are keeping yourself from investing your energies in the right approach.

Prayer

Father, please show me any place in my thinking where I'm focusing on something that is not truth. Show me with clarity my false beliefs. Then show me the truth, and I will learn to focus on it. In the name of Jesus, amen.

8

Changing to the Right Perspective

Then Nathan said to David, "You are the man!"

—2 Samuel 12:7

I had a cat named Chuck. We were great pals. I remember taking him outside for the first time and placing him in the center of a beautiful, green lawn, only to have him press himself flat to the grass and scream at me in a decidedly robust fashion. It was then that I learned that Chuck was an indoor cat and was terrified by the notion of immense space.

Another time I took Chuck outside and placed him in the fluffy, white snow. He jumped like a psychotic gazelle back to dry ground. It was then that I learned that Chuck was a summer cat and that for him, winter was best seen from a great distance. I hope it pleased Chuck that I was so teachable! I did not, however, find him to be quite so adept at getting the point.

There were two things that Chuck did that always left me wondering about him. For one thing he would frequent the room where I did my writing. My turning on the electric typewriter apparently sent him some secret message requesting his presence. He would perch himself atop my typewriter and paw at the keys as they hurled themselves at the ribbon and the paper. Each time, the typewriter key would slam itself against his paw, which he would swiftly withdraw. Then Chuck would sit there and look at me with a look of extreme consternation as if I had caused his misfortune! The other thing Chuck did involved his favorite place to recline, which was directly in front of the front door. There were two problems with this decision of his. One was that there was a high probability that when the door was opened by someone coming in from outside, he was likely to get hit by it. The second problem with this location was that Chuck felt that he owned it. That left me with many a vivid memory of friends flying not so gracefully through the air, having tripped over him on the way into the house.

Now here is my point. Chuck thought everyone and everything else was the problem. The problem was that he was making some fairly bad decisions. But Chuck could not see it. I could, but he could not. There was only so much I could do to help him.

Like Chuck, and like King David in our opening verse from the Old Testament, sometimes we cannot see what is right in front of us. Someone has to lay it all out for us. Then when we see it with clarity, as happened with David, we might experience temporary grief. But once David saw the truth and grieved it, he was able to move beyond it to great blessing. Nancy will show us how easy it is to get lost looking at the fish and not see the ocean.

Nancy

"Actually, I'm doing quite well this time around," Nancy said. "I've lost ten pounds."

"That's great!" I was glad for her, but I'd heard those ominous lines before. So I inquired a bit. "What did you mean when you said 'this time around'? Have you tried this diet before?"

"Sure," she said, "I start and then I stop."

"Have you tried other diets before, and then done them again?" I asked.

"Sure," she said. "I've been dieting all my life!" She laughed and then went on. "I'm not sure I can remember when I wasn't on a diet."

"And it wasn't always the same diet?" I asked.

"No, there have been different ones," she said.

"So when will you be done?" I asked.

"When will I be done with this diet?" she asked. "How much do I want to lose?"

"No," I said. "What I mean is, when will you be finished dieting altogether?"

"I guess I never thought about it!" she said. "I guess I figured I'd be dieting all of my life."

"Was it your plan when you started your first diet to have a lifetime of dieting, a *lifestyle* of dieting?" I asked further.

"No," she said, "I guess I just hadn't looked back to see what's happened. Maybe I need to look at this." Nancy and I did look back at her dieting, and underneath we found a number of important things. Nancy had done what many who struggle with eating issues have done.

Nancy dieted so long that it had become a lifestyle. What she had intended to be a transient adjustment in her life became her lifestyle. She went on her first diet in high school. Because she lost the weight she wanted to lose, she saw dieting as an excellent plan to fall back on if she gained weight again. That made her feel more comfortable about gaining weight. From that point, dieting and gaining weight became an ever present pattern in her life. Until she applied the material in *Reasonably Thin,* that pattern persisted without ceasing.

Nancy did not question that she had not achieved long-term success with dieting. She was not thinking about the long term. She was only thinking about the short term. She was not thinking about being finished with dieting. She was always thinking about finishing a diet and dieting again when she needed to lose weight.

Nancy had settled for a series of short-term successes that never lasted, so she continued the pattern of overeating. The chronic dieting began to slow down her metabolism, and eventually the diets became less successful. It became harder for Nancy to take the weight off. The diets became less effective, and in spite of them, Nancy began to have an apparent weight problem.

The temporary, short-term success distracted her from overall clarity and overall victory. Until *Reasonably Thin,* Nancy had invested her energy in what used to work, even when dieting was beginning to fail. She had invested such extraordinary effort in her dieting that there was little left for her to take another route. That was good news, not bad news, because this time she had to rely on God's power to make the necessary changes.

I sat down with Nancy and asked her the same questions that I'm about to ask you. Once she answered the questions and gained the clarity she needed, these were some of her comments.

"I wish I had all of the money I've invested in dealing with my weight problem," Nancy said. "I feel as if I've tried to buy my way out of it. It has been a major financial and emotional investment, not to mention all of the time I've invested. When I think about it that way, I realize that it is a major investment that hasn't profited me in the long run. It has only preoccupied me. I have to ask myself whether I would continue to sink time, emotion, and money in any other investment that doesn't pay off in a more definite way. I wonder what the Lord would say about that?" It was clear that Nancy's dieting had been a major financial and emotional drain.

Another thing we found as we looked back over her dieting behavior was that Nancy's being satisfied with transient and minimal success in her eating issues paralleled her spiritual life; she had settled for occasional depth, prompted by problems that arose in her life. It was a life of reaction, not a life of proaction.

Nancy was a slave to a lifetime of dieting, always looking for something to bail her out. And she turned to God only when she needed Him to bail her out of some life circumstance. She turned to Him when her marriage was in trouble, and when her son was ill. She had learned to call on Him only in crisis times. But He was available to her for even the smallest things; she, however, was not available to Him. She had learned to handle things on her own, in the flesh, at the expense of her own spiritual growth. If that is what you have done, then you will be encouraged to know that God is redeeming the time in Nancy's life. She cannot get back the years, but God is compounding her spiritual growth.

Nancy was cheating herself out of spiritual depth and personal victory. Seeing these truths was the beginning of Nancy's being able to conquer her destructive eating. One thing she clearly understood once she evaluated her history of dieting was this: You will not look for the solution if you think you already have it. What about you? Has dieting become a lifestyle for you?

Nancy made it through to the blessings on the other side, and is now living reasonably thin. Like the rest of us, she first needed clarity on how she had handled the problem thus far. This clarity is essential, because it is only when we see the reality of how we have handled our destructive eating so far that we will be willing to let go of the old perspective and consider a new perspective.

Let's get some general clarity on how you have handled your eating issues in the past. Take a little time and answer the questions below. The answers, when put together properly, will give you some preliminary clarity.

Exercise

What was your age when you started trying to deal with your weight problem? Age____

What was your age when you eliminated your weight problem? If you still struggle with your weight problem, put your current age. Age_____

On the lines below, listing as many as you can remember, name the diets you have tried and how many different times you have tried that diet.

(Examples: Weight Watchers, Adkins, counting calories, fasting, milk shake, bananas only, Slimfast, all carbohydrate, diet pills, weight doctor, high fiber, shots, grapefruit, protein, low cholesterol, diet wafers, starvation, etc.)

(Examples: Slimfast x 3 attempts; wafers x 2 attempts; pills x 3 attempts)

_____ x __attempts _____ x __attempts
_____ x __attempts _____ x __attempts
_____ x __attempts _____ x __attempts
_____ x __attempts _____ x __attempts

_____ x _attempts _____ x _attempts
_____ x _attempts _____ x _attempts
Total number of diets attempted ___
Total number of times diets were attempted ___

Subtract the age you were when you began dealing with your weight problem from the age you were when the problem was eliminated (or if the problem still exists, from your current age). _____ years

Now use that information to fill in the following blanks: It will show you if what you have done in the past has provided a lasting solution to your weight problem or your destructive eating. If you see that what you have been doing has not been working, perhaps that will encourage you to consider another perspective. If what you have been doing has worked to some degree, you might want to consider taking your successes to a higher level.

I have been trying to resolve my weight problem for _____ years, and I have made at least _____ attempts, trying at least _____ types of diets to try to resolve it.

King David had to start his journey back to living right with a clear view of reality. That is what we need too.

Steps to Becoming Reasonably Thin

- See that your dieting in the past has not produced lasting change, and determine not to settle for anything but lasting change.
- Determine to be open to the biblical perspective regarding your eating behavior.
- Determine to let go of any perspective that is not consistent with what the Bible says.
- Determine to endure and read on!

Prayer

Father, I'm coming to You with my heart and mind open to You and Your truths about my eating behavior. I trust You to show me the truth. Show me anything that I have bought into that doesn't reflect Christ, and lead me in a way that will glorify You. Thank You, Father. In the name of Jesus, amen.

9

Understanding the Source of Your Struggles

Who remembered us in our lowly state,
For His mercy endures forever;
And rescued us from our enemies,
For His mercy endures forever;
Who gives food to all flesh,
For His mercy endures forever.
Oh, give thanks to the God of heaven!
For His mercy endures forever.
                                    —Psalm 136:23–26

I remember once being at a restaurant and watching a young child at the table next to me. He sat in his high chair, and, in the most disjointed fashion, he repeatedly attempted to apply food to his face. Somehow, the mouth wasn't the target. The general vicinity of the face seemed to be sufficient. I was fascinated with this eating approach. It was clear to me that eating or acquiring sustenance was only part of the agenda. The rest had to do with gaining familiarity with the texture of the food when applied to the body and the speed with which it could be catapulted through the air in the general direction of someone else's face.

Of course this story I just related to you is about the

developmental tasking of a child. But adults also have other agendas attached to their eating. God is the One who gave us food. It is important that we use it as He would have us use it. The purpose of food is to provide us with nourishment and with sustenance. The problem is that food has taken on roles today that it was not intended to have.

> *We no longer eat just for nourishment. We eat to relieve emotional discomfort, to please someone else, to be accepted, and to run away from problems.*

So many factors have encouraged the overuse of food today. Food is more readily available than it was in the early years of our history. It is prepackaged and easily accessible through grocery stores, service stations, convenience stores, and department stores. Now you can eat where you buy gasoline, clothing, and newspapers. And America is known for its drive-thru restaurants where we do not even get out of our cars. Now we can eat while we're on the move. We eat while we work. We eat while we socialize. We eat while we watch TV or at the movies. And we eat alone. Unfortunately, eating or not eating has been attached by many to other and inappropriate agendas.

We no longer eat just for nourishment. We eat to relieve emotional discomfort, to please someone else, to be accepted, and to run away from problems. Some eat, or do not eat, as an act of power, rebellion, or revenge. These are but a few of the agendas that, when attached to food, become dangerous. Unfortunately, these agendas become attached to food so subtly that we are not always aware of their connection.

I think back on that child in the restaurant and his adventures with food. He was no more aware of what he was doing with food than many adults whose agendas seem easily hidden from them. Let me use Susan as an example here.

Susan

Susan came to me in confusion and concern. Her weight had been steadily increasing for some time, and she did not seem to be able to stop it. When I asked her how long this had been going on, her response was typical and telling.

"I don't know," she said. "It's just been a long time."

Those comments by Susan told me that she was unaware of what was driving her eating problem. She did not know when it began, so she did not know what agenda was attached to it. Food is not automatically attached to another agenda. That is something that happens at certain points in time, and it is typically repeated. So I investigated further with Susan.

"Have you had a problem with your weight all of your life?" I asked.

"What do you mean?" she asked.

"Did you have a problem with weight when you were in grade school?" I asked.

"No," she said.

"So you haven't always had a problem with your weight?" I asked.

"I guess not," she said.

I led Susan through a myriad of questions, as we tried together to track down exactly when her weight struggles began. We finally landed on it. Susan's involvement in the quest for the answer was helpful to both of us. It helped me find the answers I needed. And it gave her a sense of industry about finding the source of her problem. She began to feel that if she found the source, perhaps she could do something about it. These were her first steps out of helplessness. Let me comment on that briefly.

Because eating does not resolve psychological or emotional issues, any use of food to resolve them will produce negative results.

Susan felt helpless when she came to my office. That tells me that thinking that someone can help you is not what provides you with a genuine sense of capability. It is the act of involvement, the act of industry, that begins to diminish the sense of helplessness. It is not enough to have someone tell you what you need to know. You must do something with it.

Here is what we found. Susan started having difficulty with her weight when her husband joined the police force. He worked the graveyard shift, and while he was gone at night she worried about him. Would he be safe? Would he get home all right?

"During the evenings when my husband was at work," Susan explained, "I'd start to feel restless with worry and anxiety. So I'd turn on the TV to take my mind off of it, then I'd eat to calm myself. I still tend to eat when I watch TV. And I overeat when my husband is working late. I still worry when he's out at night."

Susan was eating for the wrong reasons. She had hidden agendas associated with her eating behavior. Let's take a look at them.

First, Susan was eating to alleviate the emotional discomfort of anxiety. The chemical changes that occur while eating produce a sense of emotional well-being. Without knowing it, Susan was eating to alter her mood.

Second, Susan was eating to distract herself from her preoccupation with worry. Eating gave her something to do. It was a distracting activity. It busied her hands and her mind.

But there were problems with these agendas. Food was not intended to be used to relieve anxiety. Nor was it intended to be used as a distraction from worry. Therefore food shouldn't be used to resolve those issues. Remember, psychological and emotional issues are to be resolved from a psychological and emotional perspective.

Because Susan used a physical method to deal with a psychological or emotional issue, there were negative results. The psychological or emotional issues remained unresolved, and new and different problems were created: problems with weight and destructive eating. Susan had to learn not to use a physical means to resolve any issue other than a physical one. That led her into resolution of psychological and emotional issues and eventually to living reasonably thin!

Because eating does not resolve psychological or emotional issues, any use of food to resolve them will produce negative results. The original issue will go unresolved. A second issue, a weight problem, will be created. And a third issue of destructive eating will be created. Also anxiety will be intensified. Let me show you how that works.

Because there is no resolution on the original issue, there is more intensified anxiety over that original issue. Eating now produces an added problem that brings with it its own anxiety. Now the anxiety is compounded. If destructive eating is the way you deal with anxiety (or any other emotional or psychological issue) you will eat even more destructively because you have created more anxiety and more unresolved issues. Since there is no resolution, the anxiety grows, and the destructive eating behavior escalates. That is why the problem with food continues. It is also why the original issue continues. How do we get out of this mess? First list your reasons for over- or undereating.

Exercise

Take a moment and make a list of the top ten reasons why you now or have ever overeaten or undereaten.

1._____	6._____
2._____	7._____
3._____	8._____
4._____	9._____
5._____	10._____

Do these reasons have anything in common? Let's look at some common reasons why people overeat, undereat, or eat destructively. The list is not all-inclusive, but it is a good start. See if your reasons have anything in common with these.

1. *Out of habit.* Eating destructively out of habit means simply repeating destructive eating often enough until it becomes standard behavior. It becomes second nature or automatic.

2. *In response to the attraction of environmental cues.* For some of us, seeing a fast-food restaurant or a food ad on TV, or passing by a candy machine stimulates destructive eating.

3. *To alleviate emotional discomfort.* Others of us eat destructively when we are lonely or anxious. We eat when we feel empty or depressed. We eat to calm the feelings of worry, fear, anger, guilt, insecurity, hopelessness, etc.

4. *To escape or to distract ourselves from something.* We may eat destructively to avoid something such as a project or feelings we do not want to feel.

5. *To alter our mood.* Some of us eat destructively to lift ourselves out of boredom, to calm down, etc. We eat as an activity.

6. *To avoid responsibility for growing up.* Some of us overeat so we do not have to deal with the responsibility of an adult relationship. We may undereat so we will not be seen as an adult. Again we avoid the responsibilities of adulthood.

7. *To satisfy emotional needs for nurturance or comfort.* Perhaps some of us who eat for this reason had a parent who used to feed us when we needed nurturance, and now we use the same method ourselves. Perhaps food nurtures us in the place of any other relationship.

8. *To reward ourselves.* We get something done, we have something to eat. We do well at some task, we celebrate with food.

9. *To self-sabotage or self-punish.* Some of us do not feel we are worthy or deserving of love, so we starve ourselves. For the same reasons we may overeat. Then no one will want us, and with our destructive eating we will have proven what we thought to be true: We are unworthy.

10. *To self-protect.* Some of us think that if we are overweight or underweight, perhaps no one will want us. We will not have to deal with relationships. That will keep us from being hurt by others. If we hurt ourselves first, we think we will save ourselves the pain we might feel by the rejection of others.

11. *To control or to rebel.* Eating is the one area in which no one else can control us. This is our bastion of self-control.

12. *To accommodate a fast-paced lifestyle.* We eat on the run, or we forget to eat.

13. *Because of codependence.* Some of us eat at the suggestion

of someone else. We do not know how to say no, or we feel bad if we do say no.

14. *Because of peer pressure or social pressure.* Those of us who are not comfortable with being different conform instead.

---

*I*f we are using food to resolve these issues, we are misdirecting our energies toward an inappropriate task.

Do any of your reasons fit into these categories? For the most part, food was not intended to be used to resolve these issues. If food is being used to cope with or deal with these issues, we are in error and not living with God's intended and flawless plan for our lives. That fact alone could be costly, producing self-induced misery and a life that is less than what it could possibly be. And there is more.

If we are using food to resolve these issues, we are misdirecting our energies toward an inappropriate task. In addition, we are misdirecting our energies *away from* an appropriate task. These are only some of the results of eating for the wrong reasons, eating destructively! So what do we do with all of this information?

Steps to Becoming Reasonably Thin

- Determine not to use food to resolve psychological or emotional issues.
- Remember, those who are reasonably thin do not use food to resolve hidden agendas. Generally, those who are reasonably thin use food for nourishment.

Prayer

Father, please show me any instance when I am attempting to use a physical means to resolve a psychological, emotional, or spiritual issue. Please show me any instance when I use food for anything other than nourishment. Take me forward, Father. In the name of Jesus, amen.

10

Learning from Eve

So when the woman saw that the tree was good for food, that it was pleasant to the eyes, and a tree desirable to make one wise, she took of its fruit and ate.

—Genesis 3:6

Eden holds amazing truths. As we look at some of them, you may be surprised to find the role food has played in the history of sin. You may be surprised at how directly these truths relate to your experience today. Let me show you just a few of them.

The fall of man, an act of disobedience that still has the world spinning toward its worst, involved food and eating for the wrong reasons. Food was the first vehicle of the temptation of man.

From the beginning of time, food has been an important issue. It's interesting that it was a woman who was at the center of the issue, and the man took part secondarily. Both were responsible, however.

For some reason we have failed to see the significance of women's struggle with food. We have learned to laugh at it and to accept the notion that we should learn to manage our weight problems. But it is not funny. And why should we learn to manage what ought not be an issue altogether?

The fall of man, an act of disobedience that still has the world spinning toward its worst, involved food and eating for the wrong reasons.

Let's look at this through a current lens. Who are the individuals who struggle most with food issues today? Women! But there is a growing number of men who are developing destructive eating behaviors. Just how important is this issue? I can think of no other single issue than this one that so seriously and so negatively dominates women's lives.

Let's go back to Eden and look at the specifics of Eve's eating behavior. You might find some similarities between her eating behavior and yours.

Eve

Eve ate the fruit for purposes other than those for which God intended. Yes, the fruit was good for food, pleasing to the eye, and desirable for gaining wisdom. But God had placed a prohibition on that specific tree: Its fruit was not for Eve or Adam. This clearly shows that food can be used as a test and as a tool for spiritual growth and affirmation. It also shows that, in the hands of Satan, food can be used as an instrument of temptation. It shows, too, that food can be used in a wrong manner.

If we eat as a way of satisfying anything other than the need of nurturance of the body, we are using food for reasons other than what God intended. Do you eat for reasons other than for what God intended? In what way are you similar to Eve?

Eve ate for the wrong reasons. She ate to nurture her pride, to satisfy her lust of the flesh, and, perhaps, in response to anxiety created by suspicion about God's motives. She used a physical approach to try to satisfy a psychological and emotional desire. Today we use food as a way to resolve or run away from our own psychological or emotional issues. We eat to calm our anxieties. Do you eat for the wrong reasons? We are not at all far from Eden, are we?

Eating for the wrong reasons did not work. Using food to satisfy a psychological or emotional need or desire did not work with Eve, and it will not work for us. God cares very much about *how* we deal with our weight problems, not just that we deal with them. Have your attempts to satisfy psychological or emotional desires with a physical approach worked properly and permanently?

Eating for the wrong reasons had far-reaching, negative repercussions. When Eve ate the fruit, she started a downward spiral that continues to take the world to its depths today. What she and Adam did affects all of us. Think about the far-reaching repercussions of struggling with destructive eating. First, there is the extraordinary amount of time we have invested in this issue that we could have invested elsewhere. Think of the children who struggle with weight issues and who are also distracted from the Lord's perfect plan, as we pass this issue on from generation to generation. Think of the relationships we have avoided because we did not think we were good enough to be in them, due to our weight. Think of the repercussions of dying early because our weight has become dangerously out of balance.

These questions that I have asked throughout this chapter are not intended for punishment, but rather to establish the significance of this struggle in our lives. It is a serious matter. If we take this issue of negative repercussions and multiply it by the number of Christians who are struggling with it, then and only then will we get the picture of how pervasive the problem is and how far-reaching its negative effects are. We will then get a clear picture of just how much so many are being distracted from God's other purposes. On the other side of the coin, if we as Christians choose to deal with our destructive eating in God's way, think how powerfully Christ will be demonstrated to the world! Wouldn't that be wonderful!

Food was the first vehicle of the temptation of man.

Eve ate because she wanted to do things her way rather than God's. God placed a prohibition on that specific tree; it was off-limits to Eve. God gave Eve consent to eat from any of the other trees in the Garden. He had provided for her, but she wanted to provide for herself in her own way. Eve was acting independently of God, contradictory to His purposes and in opposition to His stated will. She was acting in self-reliance, rather than in reliance on Him. She was eating in disobedience! Do you have a tendency to act independently of God and to be self-reliant in matters pertaining to food? Do you actively rely on Him in this matter? When it comes to the issue of eating, are you doing things His way or yours? Do you even know what His way is? I will show you as you continue your journey to becoming and remaining reasonably thin.

Eve's eating, like Adam's, resulted in guilt. Why did they hide themselves from God? They did it because what they did was wrong; it was disobedience. If it was disobedience, it was sin. So here in Eden we clearly see that eating for the wrong reasons is sin. Do you feel guilty about the way you eat or about the reasons why you eat? Do not deny the guilt or say it should not be there. It is there to help you get back on track with God.

Eve's eating, like Adam's, was an act of the will. Eve's eating of the fruit required a decision. It was not something that happened to her. It was something she did, and it required an act of the will. The fall of man resulting from what Eve and Adam did was self-inflicted. The fall of man resulted from a decision made by one person, followed by a decision made by another person. Think about it. Is your problem with eating a result of your decisions or something that has just happened to you? If it is a result of decisions, then it is an act of the will. Once again, Eden is very close to us.

Their eating was a conflict of wills—their wills versus God's will. God said for them not to eat of the tree. They decided they were going to do it anyway. Their wills were not in agreement, and that is where the conflict arose. That is always the nature of sin, the context of sin: our will versus His will. Do you think you are exercising your will in the area of eating? Is your will consistent with His?

In the area of eating, Adam and Eve chose their wills over His will. Whenever there is a conflict of wills and one of them is God's will, which will should we subscribe to? Always God's will! In the conflict of wills between God and Eve and Adam, they chose to side with their own wills. Does your destructive eating involve selecting your will over God's will?

After our review of Eden, I think we can define self-abuse with food as eating or not eating for the wrong reasons, not eating enough, and eating too much. All of this together we will call destructive eating behavior.

Steps to Becoming Reasonably Thin

- Determine to eat for the right reason only—for nourishment and for no other reason.

Prayer

Father, I look to You and depend upon You to prick my heart whenever I eat for the wrong reasons. Father, grant that my desires through this process be conformed to Yours. I do so want to serve and obey You. May my obedience mean love to You. In the name of Jesus, amen.

11

Jesus Understands

Then Jesus was led up by the Spirit into the wilderness to be tempted by the devil. And when He had fasted forty days and forty nights, afterward He was hungry. Now when the tempter came to Him, he said, "If You are the Son of God, command that these stones become bread."

—Matthew 4:1–3

I have working puzzles down to a science. First, I lay out the pieces that form the outer edges of the puzzle. Then, I match common colors. I will save you from any more detail, but I will say this: If you are going to tell me about how to work a puzzle, you had better really know how to do it, if you want me to respect your opinion.

Have you ever had someone tell you how to do something when they actually knew less than you did about what they were telling you to do? It would be like me telling a great singer how to sing or a great artist how to paint. It would not make any sense. Why would they listen to me when I know so little about their area of expertise?

75

Imagine someone who has never built a house, standing at the foot of a construction site with a book on how to build houses, shouting orders to the carpenter on how to hammer a nail. How do you think the carpenter would feel? I am sure he would struggle with respecting the opinion of someone who has not had his experience.

In actuality, Jesus was being tempted to take a shortcut! He was being tempted to take the easy way out—a way that would have nullified the Cross. We also will be tempted to take shortcuts when it comes to food.

There is a kind of respectful camaraderie that develops among people who have had similar experiences. They can draw upon one another for wisdom and advice. They are comfortable doing that because they know that the other person has, to some degree, walked in their shoes. To some degree Jesus has walked in our shoes, even when it comes to eating.

Let's take a look at the specifics of this situation with Jesus, as it relates to food. It is important for us to know what He was dealing with and how He handled it. As Christians, our thinking and behavior are to emulate His.

Jesus

In our opening passage from Matthew, Jesus was being tempted in regard to food. What were the temptations Jesus faced? Do you face these same temptations? What does all of this have to do with destructive eating?

First, Jesus was able to be tempted because He was hungry. He had fasted for forty days and forty nights. This tells us that hunger is a legitimate need. There would have been no temptation had Jesus not had a need that was not satisfied. It was at that moment that Satan made his approach. This tells us that unmet desires for resolving our destructive eating may leave us vulnerable to those who would try to meet them outside of the plan of God.

The temptation was not just to turn stones to bread and to eat. The temptation was also to eat at the wrong time—at a time that was not consistent with when God would have Him eat. This tells us that timing is important to God and that God cares when we eat. This also demonstrates that we may be tempted to eat, or not eat, at the wrong time, a time not consistent with God's plan.

Further, the temptation was for Jesus to use His powers as God, rather than operating from His humanity. God cannot be tempted, but man can. This tells us that God cares about the power that operates behind our eating.

And since it was a temptation put to Jesus, when it comes to food, we, too, may be tempted to use our power (flesh) and not His (Spirit).

In actuality, Jesus was being tempted to take a shortcut! He was being tempted to take the easy way out—a way that would have nullified the Cross. We also will be tempted to take shortcuts when it comes to food.

By Jesus' taking the right approach to His eating dilemma, He teaches us that God cares about the method we use to resolve our destructive eating, not just the result.

Satan encouraged Jesus to take a stone and use it for the wrong purpose. This was the temptation to use the wrong thing to meet the right need. We should be careful as well, because we may be tempted to use an illegitimate means to satisfy a legitimate need or desire.

And here is something else very interesting. Food was the vehicle of temptation used to tempt Jesus! If Jesus was tempted in this way, I think we can conclude that food may be used as a vehicle of temptation in our lives.

> *Jesus confronted the same experience with which you and I have had to contend. We can trust Him because He is God and because He has been successful in dealing with experiences similar to ours.*

All of these temptations that Satan posed to Jesus were wrapped up in the issue of food. Isn't it amazing that even Jesus had to deal with temptation related to food. Isn't it comforting to know that He understands!

Jesus had already determined what He would and would not do with His life before he encountered this temptation. Jesus dealt with His temptation by turning to the Word and acting on what it said. He counted on the Word to be more powerful than the temptation. He refused to take a shortcut. He did not do what was wrong; He did what was right. Jesus relied upon God the Father to provide for Him in His power, His time, and His way. He held to the plan laid out for Him, even though it was the plan of the Cross. His foot never left the path!

Jesus confronted the same experience with which you and I have had to contend. We can trust Him because He is God and because He has been successful in dealing with experiences similar to ours. In His humanity, Jesus relied on God the Father and the power of the Holy Spirit. He is sufficient for us in power, in expertise, and understanding. He is intimately familiar with our situation. We have no better help than His. To us the temptations would seem subtle, almost invisible, but not so with Jesus. He saw it all, and He responded righteously. He will give us the same clarity, the same power, the same success!

I would like to use Paula's experience as an example here. You may be able to see how her experience contains some of the same ingredients as Jesus' situation.

Paula

"I was doing just fine," Paula said. "For two weeks, I ate reasonably and at the times I had determined, and then it happened."

"What happened?" I asked.

"It was early afternoon, and I had planned dinner for six o'clock. But some friends called and asked me to go to the fair."

"What did you do?" I asked. I was very interested in hearing her response, as Paula was doing really well with her eating.

Paula began to read from her journal. "My life and day were completely anxiety-free, and then I got the call. My friends wanted me to go to the fair with them. My first thought was that there would be food areas throughout the fair, and that would be tempting. My reaction was, 'Oh no, I can't do that!' And then I noticed an uncomfortable feeling in the pit of my stomach. I was feeling deprived! Then I realized that I was already planning to avoid food, and that my plan, i.e., 'Oh no, I can't do that!' was causing me to think more about food. So I stopped the thought and changed it."

Paula continued. "I planned when I was going to eat—at six o'clock. I planned what other things I wanted to do until then. I decided what things I wanted to do at the fair and didn't let eating interfere with them."

There was more from Paula. "I thoroughly enjoyed the afternoon. God really showed me what the temptations were. I was being tempted to eat at the wrong time. For me that leads to overeating. So instead of worrying about resisting temptation, which would have just led me to obsess on food, I planned ways to pass the test." And she did too. She passed this and numerous other tests on her way to becoming reasonably thin! Those who live reasonably thin are acutely aware that food can be used as a temptation. They prepare ahead of time what their response to that temptation will be!

If you are tempted with food, call it what it is. It is temptation. We treat things differently if we call them what they are. If we know that we are being tempted to eat destructively and that that is a wrong thing to do, we are less likely to do it. If we just see it as eating, and not as temptation, we are more likely to do it. Think about it. Do you treat sinful behavior in the same way you treat righteous behavior? If we eat in a way that is intended to nourish our bodies properly, that is a right thing to do. If we eat in a way that we know will be destructive to our bodies, that is a wrong thing to do. Do you treat self-destruction in the same way that you do self-respect? One is to be rejected, and the other is to be encouraged.

It might be helpful here to use this exercise to take a look at how you might be tempted with food. Awareness is the first place to start. Once you have done the exercise, keep on reading and keep on taking steps to becoming reasonably thin.

Exercise

List five ways you have been tempted with food. (Examples: To use food to resolve anxiety,

to undereat as a means of control, to undereat
to satisfy my pride, etc.)

1._____
2._____
3._____
4._____
5._____

Steps to Becoming Reasonably Thin

- Never use an illegitimate means to satisfy a legitimate need or desire!
- See temptation as an opportunity to do right, not an invitation to do wrong.
- Look beyond yourself and recognize temptation as Satan's attempt to disrupt God's purposes. Then fight for the cause of Christ, and nothing else!

Prayer

Father, thank You so much for giving me Jesus, who knows my struggle with food so intimately. Please give me His vision, His ability to see when I'm tempted. Plant in my heart the desire that I will not eat what, or when, You and I have not predetermined. In the name of Jesus, amen.

12

Learning from Jesus

But He answered and said, "It is written, 'Man shall not live by bread alone, but by every word that proceeds from the mouth of God.'"
—Matthew 4:4

I have a delightful way of driving my friend Beverly crazy. I think it is some kind of spiritual gift, and I am almost always willing to use it! (I want to be obedient, after all!) I love to do jigsaw puzzles! I mean I loooove to do puzzles! Beverly does not like them as much as I do—especially if she is putting one together with me. She has this crazy idea that you should have the box top out where you can see the picture as you put the puzzle together. But, she does have a point—it is easier to accomplish something when you have the plan for how it should be done. I hate to say it, but Jesus is probably on her side. He always tells us how to handle what He allows to be placed in front of us.

How did Jesus handle being tempted in the area of food? Let me first point out just a few of the things Jesus knew before He was ever tempted by Satan. He knew what stand He would take on any and all forms of temptation. He knew who He was and what His purpose was on this earth. He knew the Word as it was in that day and time. He knew His relationship with His Father and the Holy Spirit. He recognized His own voluntary limitations.

Jesus had predetermined to obey His Father in heaven. He knew that He was sent to die for the sake of mankind. It was in His heart that He would not veer off course. He knew the words of the Law and the Prophets, so He was prepared with truth. And He knew His Father and the Holy Spirit intimately. It is because of these things that Jesus was adequately prepared for any and all temptation.

What else was involved in Jesus' dealing with this temptation about food? He accurately recognized the problem as a temptation related to food. He activated His will toward what was right regarding food. He met the legitimate need for food legitimately.

Jesus responded in the right way to an external cue (Satan, who was tempting Him regarding food). He saw the significance of a divine opportunity related to food. He responded to the temptation according to the Word. He responded from the Spirit, not the flesh, as He dealt with temptation about food. He waited for the right time to eat. He experienced victory related to food! Because of His victory, we also can be victorious when it comes to food! Let's look at Barbara, and I'll show you a bit of what I mean.

Barbara

"I went to the restaurant with them [her friends], but I really didn't feel good about it," Barbara said.

"What do you mean, you didn't feel good about it?" I asked, trying to identify her feelings.

"Well, I said yes to my friends, and then, after they left, I felt this uncomfortable feeling right in the middle of my stomach," Barbara said. "It felt like something just wasn't right."

"Why did you override a feeling that was telling you something was wrong?" I asked.

> *Once we know that we may be tempted in the area of food, then we can count on God's faithfulness to provide a way to deal with it or a way to escape.*

"Well, I just figured I could handle it," Barbara said.

"Handle what?" I asked.

"I just figured I could handle going to the restaurant with my friends," she said.

"So you did recognize that the feeling was cautioning you against going to the restaurant?" I asked.

"Yes, I did." Barbara went on. "I knew I shouldn't do it, but I did it anyway."

"What happened?" I asked. Then I added, "I'm only asking this question because I know there are consequences when we do what we know inside is wrong."

"Well, I went, and I ate all of the things I hadn't planned to. I kept telling myself to stop, but I didn't. I saw things that looked good, and I just went for it. I felt guilty when I got home."

"When you look back on the experience now, can you see ways that you could have done it differently?" I asked.

"Yes, I could have not gone with them. I could have met them after they had eaten. I could have encouraged them to go to a different place to eat, where I would not have been so tempted," she said.

What was happening with Barbara? She had an accurate recognition of the problem but chose an inappropriate response. She did not recognize her own limitations. She exercised her will in the wrong direction. She satisfied a legitimate desire (to socialize) in the wrong way (detrimental to her, with destructive eating).

Barbara responded inappropriately to an external cue (food at the restaurant). She failed to see the test (whether or not to go to the restaurant) as a divine opportunity. She responded according to the flesh, not in accordance with the Word and in the power of the Holy Spirit. Her victory was limited to learning from her wrong choice.

Compare her situation with that of Jesus and how He responded to His temptation. Jesus' situation and His way of handling it were not some overly spiritual, difficult-to-understand mysteries. His situation was inherently just like ours. His response was practical and possible for you and me. He is not asking us to do what is impossible, and we can do exactly the same as He did. It is simply a matter of choice.

Once we know that we may be tempted in the area of food, then we can count on God's faithfulness to provide a way to deal with it or a way to escape. We know this because Jesus went through it Himself. He did this so we could turn to Him, knowing that He understands. It is Jesus Himself who provides us with the practical blueprint of being reasonably thin. "No temptation has overtaken you except such as is common to man; but God is faithful, who will not allow you to be tempted beyond what you are able, but with the temptation will also make the way of escape, that you may be able to bear it" (1 Cor. 10:13).

Following His practical example was part of how Barbara progressed on her road to becoming reasonably thin. This is how it can be with you, too, on your own journey.

Steps to Becoming Reasonably Thin

- When it comes to food, do what Jesus would do and nothing else.

Prayer

Father, thank You for Jesus, for the meticulous way that You have provided for every detail of my life, even when it comes to my eating. Point me back to Jesus every time. Help me be practiced in Him, knowing what and doing what He would and did do. Through the process of becoming reasonably thin, conform my heart more and more to Jesus. In the name of Jesus, amen.

13

The Hidden Value of Stress

When I remember You on my bed,
I meditate on You in the night watches.
Because You have been my help,
Therefore in the shadow of Your wings I will
rejoice.
My soul follows close behind You;
Your right hand upholds me.
——Psalm 63:6–8

Like David in this Psalm, I have stayed awake some nights feeling the stress of worry or fear. After I became a Christian, I found that during those stressful times I could cry out to God for help and comfort. He would provide it.

I have thought a lot about the issue of stress and, in particular, how it relates to food. I have wondered if under stress, somehow, the body generates some kind of chemical that makes food taste better. I will be interested to know, one day, if that is true. I have wondered, too, why some people who struggle with stress related to destructive eating call out to God, but seemingly fail to hear from Him.

Stress! We get up early, get to work early, leave work late, get home late, get to sleep late, so we can hurry up and repeat the process. Stress is here to stay, and it is important that we learn how to handle it. Stress is very often a contributor to destructive eating, and those who struggle in this area should understand it. Stress can be a good thing or a bad thing, depending on how we handle it. Angela is a perfect example!

Angela

I was sharing Christ with Angela. As a nonbeliever, a non-Christian, she listened with interest to my account of how Jesus Christ had saved me and given me new life. When I shared with her two verses from the Bible, her level of interest changed, as did her emotional intensity.

First, I shared with her this verse from the book of Romans in the New Testament: "For all have sinned and fall short of the glory of God" (Rom. 3:23). I explained the truth to Angela, that all people have sinned, including her. She became uncomfortable because the verse, the truth, bothered her.

Then I shared another verse with her. "For the wages of sin is death, but the gift of God is eternal life in Christ Jesus our Lord" (Rom. 6:23). I could see the tension in Angela's face. It was stress brought about by the truth. Stress or tension themselves can be healthy. What is done with them will determine whether they will be good or bad for us.

At a point later in our conversation, Angela acknowledged that she was a sinner in need of a savior. She believed that Christ had died on the cross for her sin, and she asked Jesus Christ into her life. By doing that, she had accepted Jesus Christ as her Savior and Lord—she had become a Christian. The tension Angela felt was an indicator of something in need of correction. Without that tension or stress she may have seen no need for Christ.

We can learn from this to see stress as a potentially good thing. Ensure that it is a good thing by responding with turning to the Lord. Relieve the stress with faith and acting on the truth.

How to Deal with Tension Related to Food

When we feel tension related to food, we need to recognize tension as an entity in itself. We need to see the tension as an indicator of something in need of correction. And we need to find the source of the tension and determine the truth behind it. Then we should act on the truth appropriately. Let me give you an example of how to handle tension related to food.

> *Stress is like an indicator on the dashboard of your automobile that tells you that your oil is low. Either we respond to it by resolving the issues underneath the stress, or the stress will become a problem of its own.*

Let's say you see a big, juicy slice of chocolate cake. Tension begins to develop. Take the time to recognize the tension. It is a feeling of slight discomfort, a feeling of wanting. You know it when you feel it. Instead of going for the cake, see the tension as an indicator of something in need of correction.

Take the time to find the source of the tension. Ask, "When did this feeling start?" It started upon seeing the cake and grew with wanting the cake. Then the tension grew even greater with your internal deliberation about whether or not you should have the cake. Determine what the truth in this situation is: "Does eating this cake fit in with what I have determined to do to eat reasonably?" Then act on the truth. Eat or do not eat depending on what you determine the answer to the previous question is. If you are not going to eat it, then do something else, and remind yourself of your planned meal later on. If you handle tension in this way you will succeed. Your faith will grow, and God will be glorified.

When stress occurs, it is important to locate and eliminate its cause. Stress is like an indicator on the dashboard of your automobile that tells you that your oil is low. Either we respond to it by resolving the issues underneath the stress, or the stress will become a problem of its own.

Those who live reasonably thin see stress as an indicator. They look for the problem underneath the stress, eliminate the problem, and by doing so, eliminate the stress! You can do that too!

Steps to Becoming Reasonably Thin

- Allow stress or tension to serve as an indicator only.
- Never allow stress or tension to exist one moment longer than it takes to resolve the underlying issue.

Prayer

Father, please bring me double good out of any stress or tension I experience. Help me use it to turn to You and to alert me to underlying issues that are in need of being resolved. I will then pursue the resolution of those issues. In the name of Jesus, amen.

14

The Subtle Motivator of Stress

And it came to pass, when she pestered him daily with her words and pressed him, so that his soul was vexed to death, that he told her all his heart.
—Judges 16:16–17

$\mathcal{A}$ny mother will be able to tell you about the pressure of a child's perpetual questioning. "What are you doing, Mom?" "Who's on the phone, Mom?" "Can I have something to eat, Mom?" "Can you come here, Mom?" "When's Dad coming home, Mom?" "Could you help me with my homework, Mom?" "Will you, will you, will you . . . can I, can I, can I?" Yikes! The irony is that when Dad comes home he cannot understand why Mom has given in to the child's demands! It is very simple. She has been worn down.

Delilah pressured Samson repeatedly for the secret of his strength. Over and over again, she tried to trick him into revealing to her the very thing with which she could destroy him. At one sad point he gave in to the pressure and sealed his fate. He gave in to stress.

Stress is a motivator. It exacts pressure. We will either give in to it or seek to eliminate it. We relieve our stress through prayer or working out at a gym. We distract ourselves from stress with TV or by reading a book. We give in to our stress and act out in anger, or we quit. The only thing that we cannot do with stress is *nothing*. The only thing it will not do is leave us alone.

It is important for us to know how stress relates to food. Since stress is a motivator, we need to know the mechanics of how it motivates us. If we know how it works, we can determine the best way to handle it. Let me give you an example using Sandra's story.

Sandra

"Whenever I go out with my friends, we always eat," Sandra said.

"Is that what you want to do?" I asked.

"Sometimes yes, sometimes no," she responded.

"Why do you eat when you don't want to?" I asked.

"Because everybody else is eating. It's the way we socialize. I'd feel odd if I didn't eat too," Sandra explained.

"You said you don't always want to eat when they're eating." I went back to her earlier statement. "That is an individual issue, not a group issue. The first thing I'll recommend is that you give yourself permission not to eat."

Sandra agreed to do that, and then I went on. "Do you recommend other ways of socializing other than eating?" I asked.

"No, not really. It always starts with someone saying, 'Where are we going to eat tonight?' Then we talk about dinner," she said.

"I recommend you suggest socializing that incorporates food less of the time and, at times, not at all. Or meet with your friends before or after dinner." I made these recommendations so she could ease out of the current style of socializing.

Then I continued. "You said you felt odd if you didn't eat with your friends. In your mind, is it OK for you to be different?"

"I don't like to stand out from the crowd, if that's what you mean," Sandra said.

"So the way you deal with the emotional discomfort of being different is to give in to someone else's ideas and avoid being different?" I asked.

It is important for us to know how stress relates to food. Since stress is a motivator, we need to know the mechanics of how it motivates us. If we know how it works, we can determine the best way to handle it.

"I guess so," she said.

By conforming to the stress of peer pressure about eating, Sandra gave up an opportunity to be real. She engaged in destructive eating and reinforced it. She contributed to her low self-esteem.

When Sandra refused to give in to peer pressure, she reversed all of the negative results I just listed above. Learning to live reasonably thin impacted Sandra's spiritual growth, her self-esteem, and her weight! You will find that it will do the same for you too!

How to Handle the Stress
of Peer Pressure

Here are the guidelines I gave Sandra regarding handling the stress of peer pressure to conform: Recognize the stress—the feeling of emotional strain or discomfort, typically accompanied by anxiety. Determine when the stress began, what was being said, done, or thought just prior to the feeling. Determine the reason for the stress: Why did you feel uncomfortable? Was it because you were being asked to do something you really did not want to do? Were you feeling pressured to do something you really did not want to do? Determine if what you are feeling pressured to do is the right thing to do: Is it right to harm yourself in order to be with others? Is it right not to assert yourself appropriately with your friends? Is it right to pretend that this is what you want to do, when in fact you do not want to? Will what you are about to do, eating when you do not want to, bring glory to God? Do what is right. Let's look a bit more at stress related to food. Here's an exercise to get you started.

Exercise

List the top five reasons why you do now or have ever over- or undereaten. (Examples: to relieve anxiety; for comfort; to relieve boredom; to punish myself)

1._____

2._____

3._____

4._____

5._____

Now, let's look at a list of the most common reasons people over- or undereat, and see if they are stress related. See if you relate to any of these reasons.

Out of Habit

A habit has an emotional pull to it. When there is resistance to the habit, it creates stress. If you are used to stopping at a certain fast-food place on the way home, you are likely to feel an emotional tug in that direction as you drive by. This stress actually encourages you to go into the fast-food place for relief from the stress. Is it any wonder that fast-food places are so successful? It is not just about their availability. It is about our susceptibility to stress and our desire to be stress-free.

In Response to the Attraction of Environmental Cues

Many of us find ourselves on the way to the refrigerator during TV commercial breaks. This is especially true when TV commercials are advertising food products. They create a mental suggestion to eat. This desire for food and the awareness of not having it at that moment have a way of producing stress. We then eat to relieve the stress.

There are some people who watch TV and notice the commercials related to the American lifestyle. They see near perfect bodies and compare themselves negatively to those bodies. Wanting to look like the ideal, they refuse to eat. In extreme cases, they may binge in response to the food commercials and purge themselves in response to the ideal body images they see on the screen. Stress is a part of the package.

To Alleviate Emotional Discomfort

When we eat, chemical changes occur within our bodies that create temporary feelings of well-being. Emotional discomfort is stressful by nature. It gives us a sense that all is not well. That sense is contrary to what we want. Stress is created when both of those feelings exist simultaneously. We try to resolve this discomfort because it unsettles our preferred sense of comfort. Some seek to relieve this discomfort of stress by altering it chemically with food.

To Escape or to Distract Ourselves from Something; To Alter Our Mood

Food provides something to do, something that is pleasurable to experience and socially acceptable. It provides a powerful distraction from boredom or work. The stress related to escape occurs when a desire to get away from something emerges. The stress grows when that desire is encouraged with more thought. The more thought that is given to escaping, the more stress is manufactured. The more stress there is, the more likely someone is to eat to relieve it.

To Avoid Responsibility for Growing Up; To Self-Sabotage or Self-Punish; To Self-Protect

For some, the stress of taking on adult responsibility seems overwhelming. The thought of it is unwelcome. For others, there is the lingering internal message that they are bad or unworthy of anything good. Some do not eat, hoping to secretly disappear. Others overeat to disappear. Both are responding to emotional stress by using food.

To Satisfy Emotional Needs for Nurturance or Comfort; To Reward Ourselves

The absence of emotional encouragement or emotional connection creates a vacuum of walls made of anxiety and tension. Eating then becomes a way to silence the silence within. The chemical changes that occur when eating feel good. They become substitutes for the nurturance and comfort that we all need from people. A dependency develops as a result of relieving stress—a dependency on indulgence and food.

To Control or to Rebel

Some people have the desire to make a statement: "This is one area where I have control, and you can't stop me. You can't control me!" But this statement is made with destructive eating behavior, rather than with words. It may be a way of handling stress that is related to a relationship with a controller. It may be a way of flying in the face of public opinion. Again, stress is a piece of the puzzle.

To Accommodate a Fast-Paced Lifestyle, Codependence, Peer Pressure, or Social Pressure

These are the stresses of the clock and the clan. In stress we eat too fast, too much, too often, and too poorly. It is all stress related.

Steps to Becoming Reasonably Thin

• Never feed stress.

Prayer

Father, keep me alert to seeing my stress and seeing it as an indicator. Help me not to run away from stress. Help me work through the stress and resolve what lies underneath it. Help me not to feed stress. In the name of Jesus, amen.

15

Eliminating Stress Related to Food

Then the serpent said to the woman, "You will not surely die. For God knows that in the day you eat of it your eyes will be opened, and you will be like God, knowing good and evil."
—Genesis 3:4–5

When I got my new state-of-the-art automobile, I was thrilled to know I could open its doors and trunk from a distance. Once, when I was leaving church, I pushed the button to open the trunk from a distance. As I looked at the car, I saw a young child and his mother walking by the trunk.

The second the trunk opened the child gasped, jumped back, and turned to his mother with a look of protestation. At the same time the mother spun around and glared at the child. It was clear that the mother's automatic thought was that the child had caused this calamity. But it only took another second to see in his eyes that he was telling the truth. I have wished many times over that I had that on videotape! It was classic.

---

*L*ies frequently play a part in destructive eating. With them comes stress. The stress then turns around and encourages destructive eating. The cycle has to be broken at the point of the lie.

Have you ever had someone lie to you, and you knew it? Or have you ever lied to someone else? Do you remember the feeling of discomfort associated with it? If we do not have somewhat hardened or seared consciences, we would be ill at ease if we were lied to or if we lied.

Most parents can see in their children's eyes the dissonance that occurs with lying. That is why, when they wonder if their child is telling the truth, they say, "Now, I want you to look straight into my eyes and tell me the truth." Every child knows that their number is up when this happens!

The reason that parents, or spouses, or those closely in tune to our lives can see the truth or the lie in our eyes is fairly simple. When we know the truth and we deliberately distort it, emotional tension results. It creates anxiety, which to the discerning eye is visible and to the discerning ear can be heard.

Lies frequently play a part in destructive eating. With them comes stress. The stress then turns around and encourages destructive eating. The cycle has to be broken at the point of the lie. Let me show you how easily lies make their way into our thinking.

Joe

"Chocolate just screams out to me!" Joe said. "I just can't keep my hands off of it."

"Let me get this straight!" I said. "A chocolate bar sits on a counter in a store and screams, 'Joe! Joe!' And if you don't mind my asking, are you the only one who hears the little chocolate voices? Or do they ever call anyone else's name, like 'Edna! Edna!' or 'Philip! Philip!'? Have you ever picked up a chocolate bar that was screaming out someone else's name? Perhaps we should switch the topic to psychosis!" Fortunately, Joe had a sense of humor!

"What would happen if you just saw it as a candy bar that had no connection to you at all?" I asked rhetorically. "The stress would be gone. The stress is created in what you tell yourself. Lies create stress in a life where truth is to be the status quo. Lies create spiritual, psychological, and emotional disequilibrium or dissonance.

Learning to tell the truth about food and his destructive eating was important to Joe as he traveled the road to becoming reasonably thin. You'll need to know the truth too.

One way of defining stress is to see it as pressure or tension. It can be manifested as physical pressure: When too much stress is placed on a bone, it can break. When we stress our bodies with a lack of sleep, we can physically, emotionally, and psychologically break down. When we are at odds with God, we feel the stress of spiritual dissonance. When we are at odds with ourselves, or with someone else, emotional stress may result.

There are stresses in life that are due to actual circumstances, when perceived accurately, and worthy of presenting to God. Stress caused by real events, outside of ourselves, may require adjusting our circumstances, as well as our thoughts.

We may rationalize that stress is only in our head. That would in part be true. But, some stress is *only* in our head, and not in our outside circumstances until we put it there.

Our goal here is to eliminate contrived and unnecessary stress, as opposed to stress caused by real events. Relieving the stress that we create within our minds requires our adjusting our thinking. What we want to know about stress is where it came from and what we are going to do with it. Let's go back to Eden and look at the anatomy of Eve's stress.

Eve

Eve was under stress because of a lie. Only when Satan refuted God's statement that she would die did Eve succumb to risks she otherwise might not have taken.

Satan, a force outside of Eve, triggered the stress, but the stress was all in Eve's mind. The things Eve was told, which she believed, were not true, although there were bits of truth included. Satan said, "You will be as God." It was a lie with a piece of truth in it. She would be like God in knowing good and evil. But in eating the fruit she would be unlike God, because God never sinned.

The role of stress in destructive eating is so vast, that to conquer stress is to eliminate much in the way of destructive eating.

Eve was dissatisfied with her current condition, even though it was perfect. When she listened to Satan, only then did she become dissatisfied. In Eve we now see the rudiments of low self-esteem. "I'm not good enough as I am, as God made me."

Eve went after a right thing in a wrong way. To be like God is a fine desire, but how we go about it is the issue. Eve may, in part, have had reasonable motivation; however, she went about getting the right thing in the wrong way.

Pride may have been a motivator with Eve. "You will be like God." We are drawn to the possibility of ruling our own destinies; it appeals to our pride.

God never got what He wanted in an illegitimate way. God cares as much about the *way* we do things, as that we do things. God does not honor shortcuts. Jesus Christ came to earth as a man, went through the experience of the Cross, and is now at the right hand of God the Father, where He now intercedes for us. He did not take a shortcut.

Satan encouraged Eve to doubt God and what He said, and to be suspicious of God's motives. Suspicion and doubt both create stress. The things Satan told Eve and the things she believed—the things she told herself—were not true. They were mixed messages, deceit, a mixture of lies with some truth. We do the same thing. Christians can be deceived by others, and we can be self-deceived. Let me give you an example.

We have already eaten earlier in the day, and we are not really hungry, but we say to ourselves, "I want to eat." Yes, that is true, we want to eat, but do we want to destroy ourselves with food? Do we know that is what we are doing? Or do we deny that cardinal truth, just long enough to eat destructively? If we do, we are self-deceived.

Eve's experience and ours are much the same. Like Eve we momentarily disconnect from the truth the consequences of our actions. Then we deny truth or postpone the awareness of the things that are true. But, like Eve, we do not escape those inevitable consequences of our thoughts and actions. The truth is, we manufacture much of our own stress by the things we tell ourselves.

The role of stress in destructive eating is so vast, that to conquer stress is to eliminate much in the way of destructive eating. Do you tell yourself lies about food? That may be a part of your stress. This next exercise might help you put your thoughts together.

Exercise

List the top two lies you tell yourself related to eating.

Examples: "I have to eat everything on my plate" (creates false guilt). "I can't just eat one!" (creates feelings of desperation or deprivation). "It won't matter if I do this just this one time" (creates excitement mixed with anxiety and doubt). "I'll eat less tomorrow" (creates stress for tomorrow).

1._____

2._____

Stress can be a torment or a conductor, a drain or an encouragement. When seen for itself it is unpleasant. When seen for its godly use, it is an encouragement to turn to God. It encourages us to activate our faith by acting on the truth. That proves His Word to be true and brings Him glory.

How to Turn Stress to God's Glory

Here is how to turn stress to God's glory! Recognize the feeling of stress. It is accompanied with anxiety. Determine where the stress is coming from. Ask this question: "What was I doing or thinking just prior to feeling stress?" Determine if the cause is based on truth or lies. Tell the truth. Take proper action on the truth. In doing so you live a more righteous life, and God is glorified. And you have worked in cooperation with God to turn tension and stress to the good. Here is an example.

The feeling of stress backed by anxiety emerges. I recognize that it is stress. "What was I doing or thinking just prior to the feeling of stress?" I was thinking that it wouldn't matter if I eat this way one time. Is that true? Yes and no. Yes, it is true that it would not matter if I eat this way one time. But, in actuality, I am eating this way habitually, and that habit will lead to weight gain. So the answer is actually no, because the statement I used to justify my eating was a lie. It was a half-truth. While it wouldn't matter if I ate this way one time, my intention was to continue my destructive habit. That was the *whole* truth. What will I do with that truth? I will not eat this way, because it is a part of a habit that destroys my body.

Steps to Becoming Reasonably Thin

- Never let stress, whether externally generated or self-generated, live one moment longer than it takes to properly get rid of it.

Prayer

Father, I know how tense I can become. I know that stress plays a part in my destructive eating behavior. I look to You to make my senses vigilant to stress. Bring stress to my awareness when it is there, and lead me into the discovery and elimination of its origins. I commit myself to this work on Your behalf that there be nothing in between You and me. In the name of Jesus, amen.

16

Eliminating Eating as a Method of Avoidance

But Jonah arose to flee to Tarshish from the presence of the LORD.

—Jonah 1:3

There is no better example of avoidance than Jonah, who tried his best to avoid the inevitable and failed. In a number of basic ways, those who struggle with destructive eating are not far from Jonah. Let's draw comparisons between Jonah's plight and our struggles with destructive eating.

Jonah was God's prophet. Christians are God's children. Jonah was given an assignment. We are assigned the task of bringing glory to God. Jonah was given adequate instructions on the right thing to do. We have been given adequate instruction regarding our eating behavior. Don't do anything that would bring Him any dishonor. "All should honor the Son just as they honor the Father. He who does not honor the Son does not honor the Father who sent Him" (John 5:23). Treat our bodies as His temple, which they are. "Do you not know that your body is the temple of the Holy Spirit who is in you, whom you have from God, and you are not your own? For you were bought at a price; therefore glorify God in your body and in your spirit, which are God's" (1 Cor. 6:19–20). Present our bodies to Him as living sacrifices. "I beseech you therefore, brethren, by the mercies of God, that you present your bodies a living sacrifice, holy, acceptable to God, which is your reasonable service" (Rom. 12:1).

Jonah was equipped as a prophet to do the job. We are equipped as Christians to deal with our destructive eating. We have been given everything we need that pertains to godly living. Jonah disobeyed God. When we eat in destructive ways, we are being disobedient. When we know the right thing to do, and we don't do it, it is sin. "Therefore, to him who knows to do good and does not do it, to him it is sin" (James 4:17). When our eating behavior is enslaving us, we are going against what God has told us to do. "Stand fast therefore in the liberty by which Christ has made us free, and do not be entangled again with a yoke of bondage" (Gal. 5:1).

> *We are equipped as Christians to deal with our destructive eating. We have been given everything we need that pertains to godly living.*

Jonah tried but could not run away from God. Those who eat destructively may push God out of their consciences or put Him on hold as they eat destructively, but they cannot run away from Him.

Here are lessons from Jonah that also apply to us.

It is better to obey immediately rather than later. It is better for us to eat nondestructively than to end up dealing with the multiple negative consequences of not doing so.

Jonah's disobedience affected others: the crew of the ship and the Ninevites. Our destructive eating—our disobedience—affects us individually, our witness, and those who care about us.

Jonah's obedience affected others. Our obedience will affect us individually and will affect our witness. It will also affect our relationships with those we care about. God's plan will succeed. We will be conformed to His image eventually, but better now than later. God's grace includes more than just us. We are to be concerned about not only ourselves, but about others we impact with our destructive eating, and those we would impact with our disobedience.

God may give us a task that we may not want to do or that we may think we are unable to do, such as conquering our destructive eating. We may, for a period of time, think we are actually getting away with running from what we know to do, but God's patience is not the same thing as approval. Like Jonah, we can contribute to our own discomfort. Like Jonah, we can become victorious. Lydia is a good example of how subtle using food for avoidance can be.

Lydia

Lydia did not seem to know how to sit on the living room sofa without having food to eat. I asked her about her avoidance. Here is part of the conversation.

"I don't like to sit and do nothing," Lydia said. "So I do something else or just eat."

Lydia was eating as a way of avoiding sitting and doing nothing. I asked her why she was doing that. She said it was because she felt guilty unless she was doing something.

I asked her why, and she replied, "We weren't allowed to just sit and relax in our home. Mom would say, 'Don't just sit there! Get up and do something productive!' If we just sat there and relaxed, she'd tell us we were lazy, and she'd get on our case."

What Lydia was experiencing was "conditioning" from her childhood. Keeping busy became a way for her to avoid guilt and negative repercussions from her mother. That set her up to be in a mild state of "perpetual motion," because slowing down induced guilt.

Lydia knew intellectually that she didn't have to be working all of the time, but that perpetual motion factor was still at work. She could sit and not work, but she was unable to sit and relax. So she did what she enjoyed: She ate destructively. And the eating calmed her; she had conditioned herself to use food as a calming agent.

Avoidance is coping. Avoidance is surviving. Dealing directly with what you would previously have avoided is living.

Lydia had dealt with the issue of not always having to be productive. But she had not dealt with the issue of being perpetually busy. She then had several things to do. She had to disconnect eating from relaxing and see them as separate experiences. She had to find out what her perpetual motion was helping her avoid. She had to resolve the avoidance issue and dismantle the destructive eating.

Once we found out what the issues were, we worked together in a way that helped Lydia move beyond those issues and on to becoming reasonably thin! Since dismantling destructive eating is the objective throughout the entirety of *Reasonably Thin*, let me show you some pointers on how to track down issues of avoidance related to food.

Tracking Down Issues of Avoidance

First, acknowledge that eating for you is an activity. Then seek to find what this activity is replacing. Ask this question first: "I'm eating instead of doing what?" Then ask, "Why am I avoiding whatever I could be doing instead of eating?" Refuse to use food to resolve these issues, and resolve them appropriately. Here are some examples of using food to avoid other issues.

• *Eating to Avoid Feeling Alone.* Food takes on the attributes of a companion. It is there with us. It is consistent. It is nurturing. It is faithful. Replace the relationship you have with food, with relationships with people. Make friends through church, serve people, etc.

• *Eating to Lift Ourselves out of Boredom or Fatigue.* Food becomes a mood-altering substance and an activity. Instead of using food, alter your mood appropriately: exercise, join a gym, take a walk, serve people, etc.

• *Eating to Numb Our Feelings of Pain.* Again, food is a mood-altering substance that numbs our feelings and saturates our senses. Talk to someone, serve people. Work through and talk through your feelings, do not numb them.

- *Eating as a Way to Avoid Socializing.* Avoiding socializing is a way of avoiding feeling uncomfortable in a crowd. Develop real interest in other people, focus on them instead of your own discomfort.

- *Eating as a Way of Avoiding Responsibility.* Avoiding responsibility is as a way of avoiding the fear of failure or success. Accept responsibility instead.

- *Eating as a Way of Avoiding Marital Sex.* Avoiding marital sex is a way of avoiding emotional intimacy. If necessary, see a counselor once you have determined what you are avoiding. No longer use food to avoid these issues. Appropriately resolve the issue you have been avoiding.

We can avoid unpleasant tensions to such a degree that avoidance can eventually become automatic. Avoiding what we do not want to deal with exacts a great price. Avoidance is coping. Avoidance is surviving. Dealing directly with what you would previously have avoided is living. If you have subscribed to a life of avoidance, dealing directly with your uncomfortable tensions will not be automatic. It will require a choice. Eventually, choosing life instead of avoidance will become your automatic tendency.

Steps to Becoming Reasonably Thin

- Recognize what you are avoiding by eating.
- Never use food as a justification or excuse for avoidance.
- Recognize that avoidance robs you of the opportunity for growth and life.
- Never avoid what can be resolved!

Prayer

Father, please show me what I have been avoiding. Help me face these things directly so that I don't run or hide. Help me find life in places where I have been satisfied with coping. I'm listening, Father. Please shine Your light and show me any instance where my eating is a way of avoiding dealing with real life. I want to be real for You. In the name of Jesus, amen.

17

Eliminating Hidden Motivators

Then Naaman went with his horses and chariot, and he stood at the door of Elisha's house. And Elisha sent a messenger to him, saying, "Go and wash in the Jordan seven times, and your flesh shall be restored to you, and you shall be clean." But Naaman became furious, and went away and said, "Indeed, I said to myself, 'He will surely come out to me.'"

—2 Kings 5:9–11

I remember, as a child, really enjoying the use of a flashlight. It allowed me to see things that I could not have seen otherwise. I would shine it on the wall at night and make the outline of a bird's face with my hands. I would shine it in the tall weeds behind my grandparents' house to see if there was some secret path for me to follow.

The flashlight was a wonderful adventure to me. It opened up a world of wonder and excitement. I would take it into the closet in the attic where my grandfather's old World War II memorabilia was stored. There I would imagine the heroics of the soldiers and the broken hearts they left behind. OK, I confess to being a romantic!

Just as the flashlight could shine into places of darkness and expose what was hidden, so can the light of His Holy Spirit shine on our innermost thoughts. He is truly wonderful! More wonderful than the flashlight.

The things we keep out of our awareness because of the discomfort they cause us are the things we should expose. Our efforts at hiding them keep us from being authentic and free. These things are difficult to see because we have avoided the awareness of them so well. But nothing is so hidden that God cannot see, and He is willing to show us what they are. He is willing to shine the light of His Holy Spirit on these forgotten issues. When He does, we can seek resolution for these encumbrances.

In our Old Testament verse, Naaman's hidden motivation of pride was exposed. Because of his pride, he came close to missing life. His pride was hidden beneath his behavior, motivating his anger and self-sabotage. Some of us act on hidden motivation. In the area of destructive eating, this is quite common. Let's look at Gloria and see how this works with destructive eating.

Gloria

"I don't know why I do it," Gloria explained. "It seems so automatic."

Gloria did not know what drove her eating behavior. It had been a long time since she had come into conscious contact with her hidden motivation. But that motivation was the very purpose of her behavior—to numb her senses and to help her remain out of touch with the underlying reason for her destructive eating.

To enable Gloria to come into contact with her hidden motivation, I had her temporarily stop her destructive eating behavior and allow the light of God's Holy Spirit to shine on her motives. As soon as she stopped her destructive eating, a wellspring of uncomfortable emotions surfaced. She felt the loneliness and pain associated with her isolated lifestyle. Getting in touch with those emotions was a major step in Gloria's journey to becoming reasonably thin. Once she identified the feelings that drove her destructive eating, she was able to determine what was causing them.

> *The things we keep out of our awareness because of the discomfort they cause us are the things we should expose. Our efforts at hiding them keep us from being authentic and free.*

What was causing her pain was the absence of relationships she desired in her life. She wanted to feel connected to others, to be loved and accepted. She was numbing her feelings of pain with food instead of resolving them with relationships. She developed a relationship with food at the expense of people. When she began to reach out and develop relationships, these painful feelings began to disappear. So did the destructive eating. It no longer served a purpose in her life.

When we use food to satisfy a desire or need other than nourishment, we must look underneath the behavior to find what is driving it. The only way to do that is to stop the behavior. That's right. You first stop the behavior. I'm not talking here about stopping the destructive eating forever. That is the process this book is all about. I'm just talking about stopping the behavior long enough to allow the feelings that drive you to surface—that is how to expose them.

Once you stop the behavior, do not replace it with something else. This is a basic problem with diets. The eating behavior is replaced, not resolved. Only in stopping the behavior will we come to know what is underneath. We stop the behavior, wait for the feelings, find the cause of the feelings, then resolve the issues that drive the feelings. Once that is done, there is no longer a purpose for the destructive eating. There are no uncomfortable feelings to numb, no unmet needs.

How to Expose Hidden Motivation

Pray, confessing any known sin, and access God's power by requesting that He reveal to you the truths regarding your overeating/undereating/eating for the wrong reasons. Let the Holy Spirit be your flashlight.

Then stop the destructive eating behavior and do not replace it with anything else. Once you have stopped, pay particular attention to your feeling responses. They will occur in the absence of the destructive eating behavior.

> *This is a basic problem with diets. The eating behavior is replaced, not resolved.*

Journal those responses. "When I stopped overeating, undereating, or eating for the wrong reason, I felt _____. Then I felt _____. Then I felt _____." Example: "When I stopped overeating, or undereating, or eating for the wrong reasons, I felt, at first, anxious. Then, I felt anger at having to stop my eating behavior. Then, when that feeling stopped, I felt deprived!"

Once you have landed on the feelings, other questions become necessary. Most any question will do, as long as it leads you to what is underneath the feeling. Let me give you some possible questions. "Why am I feeling this particular feeling?" "Is the feeling unwarranted?" "Is it about another place or another time?" "Can this feeling be related to anything other than food?" "Am I feeling this way about any other areas of my life?"

Let me give you an example of possible answers to those questions. "Why am I feeling deprived? I don't know. What am I feeling deprived of? Food? Yes. Is that feeling of being deprived of food unwarranted? Yes, I can have food anytime I want to eat. I'm not really deprived of food. Can this feeling of being deprived relate to anything other than food? Yes. What areas? Well, a person could feel deprived of attention, approval, nurturing, financial support, relationship, meaning in life, etc. Do I feel deprived in any of those areas? Yes, I feel deprived of attention. Am I using food to meet the need for attention? Yes. I eat when I feel that no one cares about me, or when no one pays attention to me. So I also eat to nurture myself, when I don't feel that anyone cares about me. What is the feeling I have when I feel no one cares about me? I feel lonely. Do I eat to numb that feeling? Yes. So there are three reasons why I eat for purposes other than nourishment: to gain attention, to gain nurturance, and to numb my feelings. Because of that I have three times the reasons to eat than if I ate for nourishment alone!"

Once you have narrowed down the reasons, the next step is to answer these questions: "Are these feelings/needs/desires intended by God to be resolved with food?" "How does God intend these feelings/needs/desires to be resolved?"

Here is an example. "Are these feelings/needs/desires for attention, nurturance, and relationship intended by God to be resolved with food? No. How does God intend these feelings/needs/desires of attention, nurturance, and relationship to be resolved? With people."

Once these questions are answered, the next step is to develop a plan. First, determine to not use food to resolve these feelings/desires/needs for attention, nurturance, and relationship. Next, determine to get these feelings/desires/needs for attention, nurturance, and relationship resolved in a way that God would honor and that would honor God. This would be through legitimate means—through people. Then develop a specific strategy for getting those feelings/needs/desires for attention, nurturance, and relationship resolved. As an example, "I plan to call parents, friends, clergy, etc., on predetermined days and at predetermined times. I plan to reach out and give to others, volunteer my time, ask people over to my place, catch a ride with someone to work, attend a Bible study or start one, get to know my neighbors, volunteer for service at church, etc."

Steps to Becoming Reasonably Thin

- Never allow hidden motivators to remain hidden in your life one moment longer than it takes to fully expose them.
- Never let what has been exposed remain unresolved one moment longer than it takes to resolve it.

Prayer

Father, You have the power to hide things from me, and You have the power to reveal things to me. Please lay open in front of me and make clear to me the hidden motivators related to my eating. Show me what I can't see without You, so that I may praise You, and so that together we may eliminate these motivators. May Your Spirit be my flashlight. In the name of Jesus, amen.

18

Understanding the Role of Feelings

Then they sent the tunic of many colors, and they brought it to their father and said, "We have found this. Do you know whether it is your son's tunic or not?" And he recognized it and said, "It is my son's tunic. A wild beast has devoured him. Without doubt Joseph is torn to pieces." Then Jacob tore his clothes, put sackcloth on his waist, and mourned for his son many days. And all his sons and all his daughters arose to comfort him; but he refused to be comforted, and he said, "For I shall go down into the grave to my son in mourning." Thus his father wept for him.

—Genesis 37:32–35

Feelings are powerful. They grab hold of our lives and twist them and turn them, sometimes with joy and sometimes with grief. They are fiercely involved in destructive eating. Some eat to drown their feelings. Some avoid eating to avoid feelings associated with eating. No pattern of destructive eating can be thoroughly dismantled without dealing with the underlying feelings.

People ask me if feelings are real and my answer is yes.

But they may not be based on thinking that is true. This is the situation in the passage about Jacob. Jacob spiraled into an intense period of prolonged grief over the loss of his son, Joseph, to wolves. The grief was real! It was excruciating. But it was based on a lie. Joseph was actually alive and well the whole time Jacob was grieving his death.

Feelings are powerful. They grab hold of our lives and twist them and turn them, sometimes with joy and sometimes with grief. They are fiercely involved in destructive eating.

The problem with running our lives based on feelings is that feelings can be based on something other than truth. They can be based on chemicals. They can be based on lies. They can be based on only part of the truth, at the expense of the rest of the truth. Remember, feeling that something is right or wrong does not make it right or wrong.

When we choose to live according to our feelings, we leave ourselves vulnerable to lies and to parts of the truth. God, however, would have us live according to the *whole* truth and according to reason! This is why the title of this book is *Reasonably Thin*. We are to choose, in general, to live according to thinking rather than feelings, according to reason rather than emotion. We are to live according to thinking what is true, not false, and to the whole truth, not just a part of the truth. Notice how the apostle Paul says we are to renew our minds, not our feelings. That is because our feelings will follow our thoughts. "And do not be conformed to this world, but be transformed by the renewing of your mind, that you may prove what is that good and acceptable and perfect will of God" (Rom. 12:2).

People have been told to act a certain way, and the feelings will follow. This notion is one of the biggest mistakes of the recent past. Many have tried to behave their way into feelings. Wrong! Their feelings will not change unless their thoughts change. We are not told in this verse to renew our feelings or our behavior. Our feelings are generated by our thoughts. Our behavior follows either. Because of that, it is important for us to question the thinking beneath our feelings and conform our thinking to the truth. It is also important to question the thinking beneath our behavior, and again, conform our thinking to the truth. Diedre is a good example of someone who used to live by her feelings.

Diedre

Diedre's goal was to lose twenty-five pounds so she could feel better about herself. She did not feel acceptable unless her weight was where she wanted it.

"Acceptable to whom?" I asked.

"I'm not acceptable to myself, and I'm not acceptable to others," she said.

"Whether you're acceptable to others or not remains to be seen," I said. "But could you clarify for me what you meant when you said you weren't acceptable to yourself?"

"I mean it," she said. "I don't accept myself."

"Is there anything about yourself that you do accept?" I went on. "I mean, do you accept your intelligence, your smile, your talent [Diedre was a singer]; your spiritual gifts, your compassion, your reliability, etc.?"

"Well, sure," she said. "I appreciate all of those things,

and if I looked hard, I might even squeak out a few more things. But I don't accept my weight!"

"That makes more sense to me," I said. "Does it help to remind yourself of all of those good attributes?"

People have been told to act a certain way, and the feelings will follow. This notion is one of the biggest mistakes of the recent past. Many have tried to behave their way into feelings. Wrong! Their feelings will not change unless their thoughts change.

"Yes," she said. "It does. I don't feel quite so bad."

I watched Diedre's expression soften with each attribute I listed. Her feelings were changing from desperation, to sadness, to being encouraged.

Diedre had been basing her entire acceptance of herself on her weight. Since she was dissatisfied with her weight, she was dissatisfied with her whole life. Her feelings were based on her thoughts, and they changed as her thoughts changed. Remember, by choosing your thoughts, you are choosing your feelings.

Diedre made herself feel desperate by ignoring all of her positive attributes and focusing only on the one thing she did not like. As we have seen in other areas of *Reasonably Thin*, when we focus on one thing the feeling related to that one thing will grow! We are then out of balance!

A part of Diedre's goal was to feel better by losing twenty-five pounds. First, her focus was on the problem, and her gauge for success was her feelings. Because of this, her focus was off, and she caused herself to obsess on food. This caused emotional discomfort. Because her gauge for whether or not she was successful was her feelings, her sense of self-worth fluctuated with them. Because she ate to numb uncomfortable feelings, her destructive eating increased. How did she get out of this mess? Let me show you.

How to Eliminate Emotional Domination of Your Life

Determine if your life, or any area of it, seems to be driven by feelings. Some of the indicators would be if your life seems like an emotional roller coaster, if you seem moody, if you seem driven, if you cannot seem to slow down, if your eating is diminished or excessive, or if you are unhappy.

At your first reasonable opportunity, take some time to yourself and find a quiet place where you can be alone. I know that can be difficult, but it is a must! Stop whatever you are doing. Put down the book, or the work, or the food—stop any activity. Just stay still for a while. Just sit there, and do nothing.

Listen to what your feelings are telling you. Example: "I'm so tired, or so lonely, or angry, or discouraged, etc." Identify the feelings of loneliness, fatigue, worry, etc.

Look for the thought behind the feeling by asking why you feel that way. "Why am I lonely, angry, discouraged, etc.?" Conform the thought to the truth. "Do I have legitimate reasons to be lonely? Do I have legitimate reasons to be angry? Do I have legitimate reasons to be discouraged?"

Act on the whole truth. "Yes, actually I have good friends, but I haven't called them recently, so I'll call them." Or "No, I don't actually have grounds to be angry until I find out what he really meant by what he said. So, I'll get clarity first." Or "No, I have no real reason to be discouraged. I'm

just too focused on myself. I think I'll focus on serving someone else."

By doing this, you have determined to live by reason, not
by feeling. The feelings will conform over time. Remember,
those who are reasonably thin are not dominated by feelings,
they are dominated by reason conformed to truth.

Steps to Becoming Reasonably Thin

- Look at the world through truth, and let the feelings
  follow.
- Don't look at the world through feelings, and let the
  thoughts follow.

Prayer

*Father, please realign my heart to reason and truth. Thank
You for the power You have given me to live the truth according to Your Word. In the name of Jesus, amen.*

19

Eliminating Guilt

And they heard the sound of the LORD God walking in the garden in the cool of the day, and Adam and his wife hid themselves from the presence of the LORD God among the trees of the garden.

—Genesis 3:8

I remember being at the top of a mountain trying to determine whether to ski the intermediate or advanced run. I inched toward the advanced run and while distracted adjusting my binding, I started sliding forward. My next sensation was of crashing against the waist-high, T-shaped sign that read "Advanced."

There I was astride the sign. Being on a downhill slant did not make it easy to unimpale myself. I was well down the intermediate slope when a skier passed me, laughing himself silly, and said, "Hey, did you see those ski tracks around that sign? Some nut must have hit it!"

"Can you imagine that?" I said, wishing he would just get on his merry little way!

Encountering the sign was painful, but it prompted me back onto the right path and out of danger. This is the way guilt is supposed to operate. Guilt lets us know we are on the wrong path, and prompts us back onto the right path.

We live in an age where guilt is seen as a bad thing. But guilt is a good thing when it is appropriate guilt. It is a guide-post to those who would choose to live righteously. It lets us know when we have done something wrong, or when we have failed to do something that is right. If we respond to guilt properly with confession, repentance, conformance, and forgiveness, then guilt has done its job properly and we move on. Problems come when we fail to respond to true guilt properly, or we buy into false guilt.

Guilt comes in the forms of the fact, and the feeling. There are cases where people are guilty of sin, but their con-sciences are to some degree hardened, or for some other rea-son they do not feel guilt. Some people justify their behavior to try to avoid the feeling of guilt, or they deny the behav-ior for the same reason. They are still guilty, but they do not feel guilty.

> *We live in an age where guilt is seen as a bad thing. But guilt is a good thing when it is appropriate guilt. It is a guidepost to those who would choose to live righteously.*

We see this with destructive eating, when we try to place responsibility for our behavior elsewhere. For example, we might say, "I couldn't help it! I ate because everyone else did!" If we make up reasons that seem to justify our behavior, even though we are guilty, we can trick ourselves into not feeling guilt. Let's call this what it really is, self-deceit. Those who are reasonably thin do not engage in self-deceit!

The longer we avoid doing what God would have us do the greater the pain and the longer the recovery. You will suffer in rebellion, being vulnerable to discipline, or you will suffer temporarily for righteousness' sake. Those who are reasonably thin have learned to suffer for the right reasons only!

We avoid the feeling of guilt because it is an uncomfortable feeling calls for a response. When it comes to eating destructively, we must acknowledge that this is wrong and change the destructive eating behavior. Why do we run from the guilt associated with destructive eating?

We run from guilt related to destructive eating because the feeling alerts us to the need for change in behavior, and we may not want to change it. Some who eat destructively do not want to give it up. They try to avoid the guilty feelings because they do not intend to change. For them guilty feelings are only reminders of their choices to rebel.

This rebellion results in significant, self-inflicted pain. The longer we avoid doing what God would have us do the greater the pain and the longer the recovery. You will suffer in rebellion, being vulnerable to discipline, or you will suffer temporarily for righteousness' sake. Those who are reasonably thin have learned to suffer for the right reasons only!

We run from guilt related to destructive eating because

we may feel that we are not able to change. You can change and God has already equipped you to do so. *Reasonably Thin* is all about helping you understand how God has equipped you, and how you may activate His power in this struggle with destructive eating. Read, reread, and read again *Reasonably Thin*, and act on the Biblical principles, and you, too, will join the rest of us who are reasonably thin. Those who are reasonably thin have learned to endure!

We run from false guilt related to eating because the feeling is uncomfortable. In this case, we are actually running from the feeling of guilt—a feeling not based on fact. A significant number who struggle with destructive eating are plagued not only with real guilt, but also with false guilt that has no basis in fact.

When we succumb to false guilt, we suffer unwarranted feelings of guilt. This makes it difficult for us to know what is true guilt, and what is not. It creates a sense of hopelessness, and pain is magnified. We must take care to determine if the guilt is real or false. They are to be treated differently. Let me use Randi as our example here.

Randi

Randi came to me at the request of her husband.

"I don't care what people think!" Randi said. "It's my business how I eat!"

"It doesn't bother you, that you're causing yourself great harm physically, emotionally, and spiritually?" I was very sad to hear what Randi was saying.

"No," Randi said, and she chuckled. "I like food, and it doesn't bother me that I eat the way that I do!"

Randi was an example of destructive eating related to rebellion. It was possible that she felt guilt, but it was so remote there were no signs of it. Randi's insistence that her destructive eating was OK was her way of avoiding the feeling of guilt. For Randi to become reasonably thin, she had to stop denying her guilt and deal with it properly.

Some who struggle with destructive eating eat too much at one sitting (eating more than they had planned to eat). They eat, in one sitting, too much food that is extremely high in fat or sugar content (eating the wrong thing). They eat something they had not intended to eat (opportunistic eating).

These behaviors may produce true guilt, a feeling we should feel when doing something that is bad for us. Let me make a few clear statements about eating destructively and sin. Being overweight is not a sin. But choosing to eat destructively is. And choosing not to eat in a way that you know is right for you is sin.

Some who eat destructively see guilt everywhere. They see a cream puff and feel guilty. This is false guilt. Temptation is not the same thing as sin. If we do not give in to temptation we have no reason to feel guilty. In fact, if we do not give in to the temptation we have just passed a test and have reason to rejoice.

Guidelines for Handling Guilt

Recognize that you are feeling guilty. It is an uncomfortable feeling backed by anxiety. Ask this question to find the source of the guilty feeling. "What am I guilty of?" If the answer does not come, then ask these questions to track down the source of the feeling. "When did this feeling start?" "What happened right before I felt the feeling?" "What was I thinking, doing, or saying right before the feeling?"

If you find that you have done something wrong, deal with it properly with confession, repentance, forgiveness, changed behavior, restoration, etc.

If you do not find that there is something you are guilty of, dismiss the feeling as false guilt. Pray that God would show you clearly if there is a problem you are not seeing. If He does not, then refuse to dwell on or to buy into the feeling. Lift it up to God, and leave it with Him. You might use this prayer as an example, "Father, I lift this feeling of guilt up to You, and leave it with You, please take it from me. I leave my heart open to Your showing me at any point where I have done something wrong. In Jesus' name, amen."

If the answer to the question "What am I guilty of?" is "Nothing" after praying a prayer such as the one above, consider that the end of it.

Steps to Becoming Reasonably Thin

- Never let false or true guilt live a moment longer than it takes to properly get rid of it.

Prayer

Father, thank You for using guilt in my life to keep me on the right path. I will listen to You. I long to eat in such a way that is responsibly guilt-free, knowing that even there, I'm honoring You. I'm living with my heart wide open to You. I want to be able to hear even a whisper from You. In the name of Jesus, amen.

20

Conquering
Fear

*For you did not receive the spirit of bondage
again to fear, but you received the Spirit of
adoption by whom we cry out, "Abba, Father."*
—Romans 8:15

I remember a tennis tournament long ago. I had made it to the final round. I was just fine until I approached the courts and saw my opponent in her letter sweater. She had lettered in tennis! In our school you didn't letter in sports, you just did them all. It was called physical education. On her letter sweater were medals and ribbons for her previous championships. *Good grief!* I thought. *It's General Patton!*

I had been successful, winning matches all day, but when I saw her dreaded letter sweater, I talked myself into massive fear! My fear affected my playing until she called a ball out that was in. With that, she stepped on my sense of fair play, and I squished her like a little bitty bug! I could have beaten her all along. My fear was totally without foundation—like many of my other thoughts back then.

The point is that fear can, at times, be unfounded. And, that unfounded fear can negatively affect us. If we fail to check whether or not the fear is backed by the whole truth, we may end up acting on something that is only worthy of being dismissed. Remember, unfounded fear evaporates when exposed for what it really is—unfounded!

> *To the degree that you choose to generate contrived fear, you are choosing to live in distorted reality.*

Contrived fear exists in our minds. Let me see if I can give you a way to understand what I am saying here. Shut off your imagination and your senses of sight and hearing. Then go to a monster movie, and see if it scares you. Be sure someone else drives though! If we can bring our thoughts into alignment with the truth of God's Word, the only fear we will know will be what He would have us know. If we can bring our thoughts into alignment with the truth of God's Word, our fears would vastly diminish, and what remains would only serve us well.

> *. . . casting down arguments and every high thing that exalts itself against the knowledge of God, bringing every thought into captivity to the obedience of Christ . . .*
> —2 Corinthians 10:5

Blair is an example of how fear, mixed with destructive eating, can be dangerous. Let's take a look at her story.

Blair

Blair was afraid of being fat. In order to avoid being fat she ate almost nothing. It would have been one thing for Blair to have been concerned with eating improperly. That would have encouraged responsible behavior aimed at eating in a healthy way. But, instead, she engaged in fear and that fear encouraged more desperate measures.

Blair's fear was a choice, and she held on to that choice because it worked. When you fear something you are less likely to be involved in it than if you simply would prefer not to be involved in it. So, if you create irrational fear it will motivate you to stay away from the feared object or situation.

There are many problems with using fear in this way. To the degree that you choose to generate contrived fear, you are choosing to live in distorted reality. That will create a self-imposed sense of isolation, which will further remove you from fitting in with society. The longer that goes on the more you remove yourself from reality and from society. This can be a formula for Christians becoming self-deceived.

The deception in this case would eventually be that eating anything at all would be a bad thing to do, and must be avoided at all costs. The cost will certainly be the abdication of abundant life. In the long run it may be the destruction of life altogether. Here another dependency was formed. Blair had developed a dependency on a lie. While fear can motivate someone not to eat, that is not the whole truth. The whole truth is that fear unchecked can lead to extreme repercussions including death.

The battle Blair and I fought together was against the use of fear as a motivator. Fear had become her insurance that she would not become fat. There was a huge payoff for her fear. In her mind to let go of her fear would have meant that she would become vulnerable to becoming fat. To hold on to her fear meant that, in time, her physical systems would break down.

> *If we do not prevent undesirable results in a responsible way, fear may rush in to maintain the distance between us and the undesirable result.*

Blair was using an illegitimate means (fear) of satisfying a legitimate desire (to be reasonably thin). In doing so, Blair was robbing herself of assuming the proper responsibility for her health, and robbing herself of the privilege of growing up. Because she used fear as the motivator, she did not develop other reasonable methods of eating.

The lack of those healthy methods left Blair dependent on fear, which turned into fear of food, and eventual terror. She began to hate food, which she needed in order to live. That created confusion and self-hate. Her body would demand that she eat and her fear would condemn her if she did. That distorted reality became Blair's only reality.

This is the kind of situation that can tear your heart apart. I felt a great deal of that as I dealt with Blair and others who have struggled with this type of destructive eating. First, I had to find my way into her reality. Then, I had to give Blair something else to hold on to. Something that she would feel secure with—as secure as she felt with fear. It was a very difficult process helping her release fear as she began to grab on to truth. Few people know the heartache felt here by those who struggle this way and by those who love them. Sometimes we have to carry them until they can walk on their own.

Once Blair finally felt safe with truth she began to transform her life. In time she determined to use only legitimate ways of becoming reasonably thin, and that began to be within her reach!

If we do not prevent undesirable results in a responsible way, fear may rush in to maintain the distance between us and the undesirable result. For others, the reverse is true. Their fear is the fear of failure, of eating destructively. Instead of that fear motivating them to eat reasonably, it motivates them to eat more. Let me give you an example of the cycle of fear of eating destructively.

The fear of engaging in destructive eating behavior leads to concentration on fear regarding food. That fear regarding food leads to obsession with food. The obsession with food leads to an obsessive negative self-evaluation. That negative self-evaluation encourages destructive eating behavior to comfort and calm emotional distress over the negative self-evaluation. The undesirable result that is to be avoided, destructive eating, in fact becomes the result of obsession. This is followed by eating destructively for comfort over failure. The failures were brought about by obsession with fear. This will continue unless deliberately altered. The focus of concentration should be removed from fear and what not to do, and be placed on faith and determining what to do. The definition of success should be detached from food.

Guidelines for Eliminating Fear

Recognize the feeling of fear. It tends to occur in the chest region and is accompanied by sharp anxiety. Then ask, "What am I afraid of?" "What happened or what was I thinking just before I felt the feeling of fear?" Then, determine whether or not the fear is based on thoughts that are true. Next, conform any untrue thoughts to the truth. Finally, respond to the truth according to Scripture. Here is an example.

The feeling of fear emerges. What was I thinking just before the feeling? I was thinking that if I eat this piece of cake, I'll get fat. My fear is that this piece of cake will make me fat. Is that true? No. Becoming fat requires repeatedly overeating over time. So, this one piece of cake will not make me fat, but if I develop a habit of doing this I will make myself fat.

God would have me respect the creation that He made. He would not have me place myself in physical, psychological, or emotional jeopardy. So, once in a while, it would be all right for me to eat a piece of cake, but making it a habit would be wrong. So, I may decide to eat the cake, as long as it is not a habit. Or, I can decide not to eat the cake and wait until another time to eat it. Either way I decide, fear need not be the motivator. The determination to honor God by eating reasonably will be the motivator.

Steps to Becoming Reasonably Thin

- Never let fear, false or true, live one moment longer than it takes to properly get rid of it.

Prayer

Father, may every fear I ever encounter turn me immediately to You. When it comes to food or any other area of my life, I acknowledge that in Your eyes I am successful. I will continue with Reasonably Thin *to bring my experience ever closer to Your truth about me. In the name of Jesus, amen.*

21

Identifying Relationship Triangles

Jesus said to him, "I am the way, the truth, and the life. No one comes to the Father except through Me."

—John 14:6

I pulled back the rubber band as far as I could and then set the rock to flight between the two sides of the wooden Y-shaped slingshot. *Quite something!* I thought to myself. *But I have no use for it. I have no desire to shoot a bird or a rabbit. I have no desire to break windows or fell playmates. What shall I do?* These were among my deeper thoughts as a child—intense, intellectual. Here was this marvelous thing for which I had no use. "This can't be!" I said to myself. And I determined to make use of it.

The rubber band with its leather pouch became the prototype for a pirate's eye patch and the bottom of the Y-shaped slingshot became a divining rod, with which I found no water at all. But at least the slingshot had a purpose and as such was valuable to me.

> *In a relationship triangle, a third party is brought into a relationship between two other parties, and that individual (or thing) serves to relieve the stress between the original two.*

I must say that I was quite awestruck at the power of the slingshot. The small triangle could be used to propel objects much farther than my arm could throw them. It seemed like such an innocuous thing. But that triangle in the hands of Charlie, the little bruiser down the street, could be a weapon. No longer would any headlight or lamplight be safe in the entire town, if Charlie had the slingshot. It was clear to me that triangles could be seen as good things or as bad things, depending on what you did with them.

Relationships are subject to triangles. What happens in a triangle? In a relationship triangle, a third party is brought into a relationship between two other parties, and that individual (or thing) serves to relieve the stress between the original two.

The verse at the beginning of this chapter reveals the greatest triangle in the Christian life. Jesus Christ died to become the bridge between God the Father and man. Christ died so that in believing in Him, our relationship with God the Father might be restored. This is a healthy relationship triangle that results in resolution. But there can be unhealthy triangles, too. Let me give you examples of a healthy and an unhealthy triangle, and then I'll show you how this concept works with food.

Healthy Triangle

Couples come to me for counseling. I become the mediator between the two of them. That creates a relationship triangle: the husband, the wife, and me. As the third part of the triangle, I help relieve the stress between the two of them by helping them deal with the stress appropriately. They find resolution, and, in the process, they learn how to find resolution without the help of a third party.

Unhealthy Triangle

Mother has a frustrating phone conversation with Dad. Once she hangs up the phone, their small child asks for a glass of milk. Mother yells at their child, "Just leave me alone!" This creates a triangle: mother, dad, and child. As the third part of the triangle, the child serves to relieve stress between the mother and father, but that is an inappropriate means of relieving stress. As a result, there is no resolution in the relationship between the husband and wife. The struggles in their relationship worsen. There is now a strained relationship with the child. This is an unhealthy triangle. Now let me take triangles into the area of destructive eating.

Erika

Erika had a frustrating phone conversation with her husband. As soon as she hung up the phone, she turned to the freezer and pulled out the ice cream. This created an unhealthy triangle: Erika, her husband, and food. As the third part of the triangle, the food served to relieve stress between Erika and her husband. But it was an inappropriate means of relieving stress. There was no resolution in the relationship between Erika and her husband. In fact new problems were created. When food is "triangled" into a relationship, the problems in the relationship are destined to multiply.

Here are some of the new problems that began to emerge between Erika and her husband as a result of unhealthy triangling with food. The more that problems between Erika and her husband arose and remained unresolved, the more Erika placed herself in front of the refrigerator. With every trip to the ice cream, Erika was putting on more weight. Her weight then became its own problem.

That type of eating—to relieve stress—is destructive eating because it is an illegitimate means of trying to deal with a legitimate issue. Because it is not the right method, it will not work. The destructive eating only becomes a problem in itself.

Erika's weight gain led to sexual dissatisfaction in marriage. She was dissatisfied with her body and was uncomfortable with her husband being close. He found her less sexually appealing due to her weight. Now with their sexual desires and needs going unmet, the sexual area became a problem.

When food is "triangled" into a relationship, the problems in the relationship are destined to multiply.

With her destructive eating Erika placed herself at risk for health problems, both physical and emotional. She became lethargic over time. She lost her interest in exercising. Her self-esteem diminished rapidly, and depression began to set in. Recreational time together with her husband began to diminish as Erika gained weight. She became inhibited about going to the beach, which had been one of their favorite things to do together. Her failure to get her weight under control led to her husband's having diminished respect for her. Because of that, she saw his love as conditional, and her respect for him diminished.

The growing dissatisfaction in the relationship led to increasingly more emotional distress for Erika: more serious depression, anger, resentment, disappointment, and guilt. Meanwhile her husband was experiencing anger, resentment, and rejection. Increased dissatisfaction with the relationship resulted in arguments and silence. There began to be increased emotional distance and feelings of loneliness even though they were married. The emotional distance began to turn into emotional estrangement.

My objective with Erika was to help her detriangle food from her relationship with her husband. For a short while, as her counselor, I took the place of food and became the transitional third part of the triangle. Once I was in place, I helped Erika face all of the problems she had avoided by using food. We dealt with those problems, one by one, until they were resolved without the use of food.

Once Erika learned to detriangle food from her relationship with her husband and to resolve the issues between the two of them, she began to build a strong and stable relationship with him. She no longer turned to food as a way to relieve stress because she now had her husband to talk to. All of the negative results of triangling food into their relationship disappeared over time, and Erika joined the ranks of the reasonably thin. Here are a few pointers on detriangling food from relationships.

How to Detriangle Food from a Relationship

How do you "detriangle" food from a relationship? Replace food, in any triangle, with any third party that will contribute to healthy resolution between the two original parties. Make sure that the third party will not create additional problems or unrighteous dependencies.

An appropriate third party will not encourage dependence on themselves to resolve issues between the original two. An appropriate third party will facilitate as the original two resolve their own problems. An appropriate third party will not draw themselves inappropriately into the problem; rather, they will view the problem from a more objective distance. Third parties may be friends, counselors, pastors, family members, etc.

Steps to Becoming Reasonably Thin

- Never allow food to be triangled into any relationship.

Prayer

Father, please guide me into a life in which all relationships are righteous. It is my heart's desire that food not take the place of any human connection. Please help me build righteous relationships with people and things, so that You are honored. In the name of Jesus, amen.

22

Avoiding Triggers

Therefore, when Saul saw that he [David]
behaved very wisely, he was afraid of him.
—1 Samuel 18:15

Saul, the king of Israel, was feeling threatened by the growing popularity of his greatest warrior, David. David's repeated successes became the trigger for Saul's rage. The more Saul encountered the trigger, the angrier he became. Eventually Saul launched an unsuccessful plot to kill David. Like Saul, we are subject to the effects of triggers. This is especially true when it comes to destructive eating.

A trigger is something that prompts a reaction. When you pull the trigger of a gun, the bullet is launched. When the clock says five o'clock, we leave the office for home. Triggers may be physical, emotional, or psychological. Something becomes a trigger by being repeatedly paired with something else. In simple terms, when we are triggered, we respond to that trigger with some type of action. If we respond repeatedly to a trigger, we may then make ourselves vulnerable to its influence.

If I see a car coming at me on the highway, it is likely to trigger fear in me, and I am likely to respond by getting out of the way of the oncoming car. In this case the trigger was visual and material, and it triggered emotional, psychological, and physical responses.

If I see in the newspaper that my favorite department store is having a year-end sale, that newspaper announcement might trigger my desire to shop, and I may then head for the store. This case has a visual and material trigger that stimulated an emotional, psychological, and physical response. You can see by these examples that triggers may be multifaceted, and so may be the triggered responses.

In simple terms, when we are triggered, we respond to that trigger with some type of action. If we respond repeatedly to a trigger, we may then make ourselves vulnerable to its influence.

Triggers are a major part of our society. Political campaigning is intended to trigger specific voting behavior. Perfume is designed to trigger a sense of pleasure. Depending on who you are and what you do, the sight of a law enforcement agent will trigger either a sense of well-being or an urge to run. Why do you think that there is advertising? It is because advertising works as a trigger to prompt the action of purchasing. Let me give you a couple of examples.

Imagine that it is a warm summer day, and you are out in the hot sun driving somewhere in your car. An advertisement comes on the radio that broadcasts sounds of the effervescing bubbles of some type of soda. That sound triggers the visualization of someone drinking a soda and finding needed relief from the heat. That visualization triggers thirst. That thirst triggers the desire to drink a soda. That desire triggers the action of stopping at a drive-thru and purchasing a soda. We might call these chain triggers, because, to put it in biblical terms, one trigger begets another trigger, that begets yet another trigger, and so on. Let's take that same scenario and see where it leads Kellie.

Kellie

Kellie has just gone through the triggers and responses I listed above. Now she is at the fast-food restaurant, at the menu where she is asked to place her order. Remember, she drove in to get a soda, but watch what happens.

"May I take your order?" the food server asks.

"Yes," Kellie said, "I'd like to have a medium soda please." All the while Kellie is looking at the menu that is directly in front of her, where, coincidentally, her head has to be turned for her to place her order. The restaurant is a visual trigger. The menu is a visual trigger.

"Anything else?" Now the food server is a vocal trigger.

"Well, yeah, I think I'll have a burger too," Kellie replies. Remember that she did not plan to order a burger when she came to the restaurant.

"Would you like some fries with that?" suggests the food server, with another verbal trigger that stimulates a visual trigger.

"Yeah, that will be fine," Kellie said. Now she has fries and a burger that she did not intend to order.

In a very few short moments, Kellie has succumbed to one type of advertising after another, all of them triggers. Kellie is now contributing to her weight problem by eating in response to excessive or inappropriate triggers, instead of eating to properly nourish herself. Because of her responses to these triggers, Kellie ate at the wrong time—when she had not planned to eat. She ate more than she had originally intended to eat. And she ate something that she had not intended to eat.

Triggers are acquired through frequent contact.

How did Kellie handle the situation in the future? She recognized and acknowledged to herself that she was susceptible to advertisements. While in the car, she kept a bottle of water nearby, in case she should be thirsty. If the advertisements on the radio began to affect her, she simply reminded herself that she would be eating later, at a certain specific time. Let's look at how triggers are acquired.

How Are Triggers Acquired?

Triggers are acquired through frequent contact. For example, when we see a fast-food restaurant and stop there often to eat, we develop a type of relationship with that restaurant. When we see the restaurant, we connect it with eating. Thinking about eating may trigger either hunger or the anticipation of eating. Stopping at the restaurant and eating may be the result.

Triggers are acquired through frequent association with

another factor. The most common of these are holidays. These can be highly specific. Just think about it. Do you eat hot dogs at Christmas or on the Fourth of July? Do you overeat at Thanksgiving or Easter?

Do people offer you something to eat when they see you feeling down? If that is done often enough, emotional pain may trigger the need for comfort, which may trigger the desire for food. If you frequently eat while you are driving in a car, the thought of being in the car may eventually trigger the desire to eat. You may then associate vacations or business trips with food. If going to the movies is fun for you, and you eat while you are there, you may associate eating with enjoyment. Scheduling a special event would then trigger the desire for food. Because of that, food is more likely to be a part of any enjoyable event.

How to Avoid Acquiring Triggers

Avoid excessively frequent contact with food. Assign specific times for *when* you will eat and places for *where* you will eat. As an example, Jillian ate three times a day, plus fruit. She had breakfast at home, sitting near her bay window at about 6:30 A.M. She ate lunch at noon, either at a soup and salad place or a sandwich shop, both near work. Between 2:00 and 3:00 in the afternoon she ate a piece of fruit or two. As a general rule she ate dinner at 6:30 P.M. in her home at the dining room table. Once or twice a month she ate dinner at a place other than home, but not more than twice. Outside of those times and scheduled grocery shopping, she did not concern herself with food.

Avoid frequent pairing of food with any specific thing. If you limit your eating with the recommendations above, part of this task is already complete. Do not repeatedly pair food

with other pleasurable experiences such as shopping, or golf-
ing, or visiting with friends. See eating as a activity separate
from any other event.

Steps to Becoming Reasonably Thin

- Assign eating to three times a day, with a piece of
  fruit or two anywhere else in the day. That will keep
  you from having to deal with the question of whether
  or not to eat and the anxieties associated with the
  question. It will also give you a structure to your eating that will allow you to look forward to the times
  you will eat. That provides assurance that you will in
  fact eat, and it eliminates the feeling of desperation.
- Remember, being proactive eliminates most of what
  is reactive. A good amount of destructive behavior is
  spontaneous and reactive.
- Remember, scheduling reasonable behavior can
  eliminate the scheduling of destructive behavior.

Prayer

*Father, help me erase any existing triggers in my life that are
related to food. Please point them out to me, and I will leave
them behind. I only want triggers that draw me closer to You
or bid me do what You would have me do. Father, keep me
alert to being consistent in the times and places of where and
when I eat. Help me develop the kind of eating structure that
will relieve me of any obsession about eating. I open up my
heart to You, Father. I'm listening. Please give me Your alert-
ness on this matter, so that I can be free for Your glory. In the
name of Jesus, amen.*

23

Conquering Social Eating

> *So when the woman saw that the tree was good for food, that it was pleasant to the eyes, and a tree desirable to make one wise, she took of its fruit and ate. She also gave to her husband with her, and he ate.*
>
> —Genesis 3:6

I could recite countless stories of those who have gone off to military maneuvers for months and ate reasonably while they were gone. And there are those who have gone on business trips or off to college and ate reasonably while they were away, only to return to destructive eating behavior when they returned home.

I could also tell you the stories of those who eat reasonably at home only to eat destructively when they are invited out to eat. At home they are disciplined and responsible, but when they are out, they lose all sense of reasonable eating.

For some, it is the context of family that causes them difficulty; for others, it is the context of friends. Still, for others it is the context of strangers or the context of a holiday event. All of these contexts have one thing in common: They are social situations.

Social and destructive eating go all the way back to the Garden and the family. When it comes to eating destructively, it is not all done within the confines of the family. And it is not all done in secret; some of it is done in plain sight. It can occur in the form of social eating. Remember, our definition of destructive eating is eating too much, or not enough, or for the wrong reasons.

> *Social and destructive eating go all the way back to the Garden and the family.*

We know that any of those behaviors can occur when we eat at times and places other than those we have proactively determined. And they can occur when we eat something other than what we have proactively determined. With that in mind, let's look at Audrey and see if that holds true with her.

Audrey

"Every time I go to my mother's house, I have the same problem," Audrey said. "The first thing she does is ask if I'm hungry. Then, before I have the time to answer, she leads me into the kitchen and fixes me food! The problem is that I don't want to eat, but I also don't want to hurt her feelings."

Audrey's situation contained a number of underlying

issues that are common prompters to destructive eating in social situations. I will place an asterisk at the end of each of those issues I list that was a part of Audrey's struggle with destructive social eating.

---

*N*ever use food as a substitute for communication or relationship.

Destructive social eating does have its complexities, but when they are sorted out and seen individually, they are a gold mine of potential growth. Here are some of the underlying issues: the perceived need for acceptance, the fear of rejection, the desire to please, people pleasing,* the desire not to rock the boat, conflict avoidance,* fear of offending, fear of appearing disrespectful,* fear of not conforming, fear of being different, the need to eat as distraction from social discomfort, eating as a bonding experience,* eating as a way of communicating love,* eating as a means of validating someone,* and eating what is available rather than what you had planned to eat.*

Each of these issues can contribute to eating destructively in a social setting. When one of these issues is compounded by another and another, as they were in Audrey's case, the more certain you can be that destructive eating will take place.

How to Stop Destructive Social Eating

What should we do with these underlying issues? After all, we do want to communicate love, be respectful, etc. The answer is remarkably simple. Acknowledge that these are the issues that you are dealing with and that they encourage destructive eating. Determine that they should be altered, so that destructive eating does not occur. Within reason, respect the intent of each of the issues. Determine to resolve the issues in a way that does not involve food. Accompany that determination with proper communication. Let me show you how that would look in practicality.

The Perceived Need for Acceptance, the Fear of Rejection

Conform your mind to the truth that you do not need complete acceptance and approval of others, even though you may want it. Allow someone to reject your behavior without that meaning they are rejecting you, the person. Then, when it comes to eating destructively, act on that truth by declining to eat. Here is how you might do that respectfully. "Thank you for the offer, but I'm planning to eat later on this evening, and I'd like to stick to that plan." At that point, draw the attention away from food and to something else. "There is something you could do for me, though. Tell me where this painting came from."

The Desire to Please, People Pleasing

Same as above. Never please to the extent that you act in any self-destructive way. Remember, our objective is to please God. He would not have us eat destructively.

The Desire Not to Rock the Boat, Conflict Avoidance

Same as the first. Remember, there is a reason to rock the boat if it is headed in the wrong direction (i.e., destructive eating). Rocking the boat is not the same thing as sinking the boat. Families, like boats, are made with a rocking motion in mind. That is how they stay afloat.

Fear of Offending, Fear of Appearing Disrespectful

Do be respectful in your declining to eat destructively. If you know that fixing a dinner is something that someone is likely to do when you visit them, let them know beforehand that you are planning to eat later on, so that they will not prepare something for you and then be disappointed.

Fear of Not Conforming, Fear of Being Different

Conform to the truth that we are all different. That is how God made us. Celebrate righteous difference, always in a respectful way. By that I mean to accept that others are different from you, not just that you are different from them. Be more concerned with eating in a way that honors God than with the notion of difference.

The Need to Eat as Distraction from Social Discomfort

Never use food as a substitute for communication or relationship. Determine to develop genuine interest in others for the sake of Christ. Never destroy yourself with food to avoid social discomfort. Strike up a conversation. Care more about who is talking and what you are hearing than your own social discomfort. Replace one with the other.

Eating as a Bonding Experience

Bond with the person, not the food. Make sure that when you are with this person, food is not always involved.

Eating as a Way of Communicating Love, Eating as a Means of Validating Someone

Communicate love in other ways. There is nothing wrong with appreciating a meal and the one who prepared it. That is a wonderful thing to do. But take great care to appreciate many other things about the person, so that they will not turn to food to please you. Appreciate their spiritual wisdom, their heart for the Lord, their communication, their humor.

Eating What Is Available Rather Than What You Had Planned to Eat

Before you return home or go out to eat or attend that social function, determine what you will eat. Be sure it is available. At home, keep food that you want to eat available. At someone else's house or at an event, determine ahead of time that you will eat only certain things that are likely to be there. Do not go outside of your self-imposed and reasonable boundaries. This way you will enjoy the social engagement and not feel guilty afterward.

Change Family Messages About Food and Weight

Since much destructive eating occurs in the context of family, let's take a closer look at family messages about food.

Exercise

List one message about food or weight that you learned from your family of origin. (Examples: "Eat everything on your plate." "Your weight should be perfect.")

_____

Now, change that same message into the message you choose to pass on. (Examples: "It's important that we don't waste food, so just eat what you want now, and we'll have leftovers later." "What is important is to eat in a way that glorifies God. It's not about weight.")

_____

List one message you have given to your family about food or weight. (Examples: "I'm not acceptable because of my weight, so you won't be either, if you're not a perfect weight." "It's OK to eat anytime you feel like it.")

_____

Now, change that same message to the one you want to pass on. (Examples: "I accept myself as a person, but I don't accept the way I have been eating destructively. So I've decided to eat three times a day, at the following times, so that I protect myself from eating destructively.")

_____

Steps to Becoming Reasonably Thin

- Remember, your environment does not control your eating behavior—you do.
- You are not out of control when you eat destructively. You are very much in control.
- If you have control over destructive eating, you are demonstrating that you can control your eating in a healthy way.
- Continue to make the right choices. Abide by the predetermined structure you have put into place that will eliminate destructive eating (eating three times a day, with a couple of pieces of fruit in between meals if desired, eating for nourishment only and at a predetermined place). With the exception of twice a month, do it no other way!

Prayer

Father, I am intent on maintaining this structure to my eating. I commit to You that I will develop this pattern of eating, so that I will not eat destructively. I'm asking You to bless this pattern of eating, that it would glorify You, as I long for my whole life to bring You glory. Please help me pass on only what will bring glory to You. In the name of Jesus, amen.

24

Enjoying
the Plateau

*Then Moses stretched out his hand over the sea;
and the* LORD *caused the sea to go back by a
strong east wind all that night, and made the sea
into dry land, and the waters were divided.*
—Exodus 14:21

It is often when our backs are
to the wall, or the Red Sea for that matter, that the best is
brought out of us and God's movements are seen with the
greatest of clarity. That is no coincidence. It is God's plan
and our privilege. When we are weak, He is strong. We are
often at our weakest when our backs are against the wall,
when we feel like we cannot go on.

When I was younger, much younger, I used to run long
distances. Many times I would approach what is called the
"runner's wall." It was that place where I felt so much pain
that I did not think I could go on. My thoughts were filled
with quitting, and each second felt like an eternity. Then,
somewhere during the thoughts, something would change,

and the pain would cease. All of a sudden, I would be able to run and not stop. It was as if I had transcended pain and had renewed energy that was more durable than it was before the runner's wall.

> *Reaching the plateau is the same thing as hitting the runner's wall. It says that we have come so far. It says that the next stage is just beyond this point. Beyond this point is a greater experience of joy, peace, freedom, and confidence. It is the place where dreams become reality.*

It was not the thinking that caused the change. I did not talk myself out of pain. It was endurance having its result. It was, and is, the reward of all of those who do not quit. It is the way we are to run the race for the cause of Christ. We are to run with endurance the race that is set before us, to bring Him glory in every area of our lives, to "grow up in all ways into Him." Each individual Christian is set on a course, a course with only their name on it. No one can run the race for them, and they are exhorted to run the race with endurance. Endurance requires an act of the will, accessing the power of God, to withstand the rigors of the race, to move ahead in it, and to win. Christians are not to simply run the race. They are to run to win!

How do we run the race with endurance? We must run with full concentration on one singular goal: to glorify God in every area of our lives. How do we do that? We do that by "fixing our eyes on Jesus." This phrase has to do with turning our eyes away from all other things and fixing them on one thing alone. This is why it is so important to be sure your goal is the appropriate goal. During the entire course of this journey we must endeavor to turn our eyes away from the symptom, away from false solutions, and fix them on Jesus.

Reaching the plateau is the same thing as hitting the runner's wall. It says that we have come so far. It says that the next stage is just beyond this point. Beyond this point is a greater experience of joy, peace, freedom, and confidence. It is the place where dreams become reality.

Every day is yesterday's tomorrow. If you keep on looking to the future, you're going to miss today!

This is the most important place for accountability. This is the best place for group support. When you have reached the runner's wall, when you have run much of the distance, that is the perfect place for sharing the next stage with a group of others who have endured as you have. What you share now are not the trials of defeat or the concerns of the struggle, but the power of freedom and the challenge of the call to the highest and best. Let's take a look at Lynette and her journey to becoming reasonably thin.

Lynette

"This is too hard!" Lynette complained. "It requires too much of me."

"What do you mean?" I asked.

"I'm tired of having to think about all of these things!" she said.

"You mean all of these things about how to be reasonably thin? All of those things that you have now been consistent with for a while?" I asked.

"Yes," she said. "I just feel so drained."

"Feeling drained doesn't make sense. Let's find out why that is happening, OK?" I knew she would agree.

"All right," she said.

"Tell me exactly what it is you're thinking that is so draining." I was looking for the error in thinking.

"I just get tired thinking of doing this for the rest of my life!" she said.

"How often are you thinking this?" I asked.

"Plenty," she said.

Lynette had nailed her problem swiftly. I'll explain to you exactly what I explained to her. Lynette was overloading today with concerns about the future. We are told in Scripture not to do that: "Therefore do not worry about tomorrow, for tomorrow will worry about its own things. Sufficient for the day is its own trouble" (Matt. 6:34). When we worry about tomorrow, we contaminate today with pressure that does not belong to today. That robs us of living life fully today. Lynette was concerned about tomorrow, when in actuality she was living extremely responsibly today.

The only issue of the plateau is endurance.

I made an agreement with Lynette that she be concerned with today only. When she complied, she was no longer drained. For her, the plateau was laden with overconcern for tomorrow. She wanted to quit, but instead she endured. She got the answers she wanted and made it through. Now she lives reasonably thin.

If you, like Lynette, can figure out the following statement, it will help you live fully today. If you can't figure it out, then never mind. You can still live fully today. Here is the statement: Every day is yesterday's tomorrow. If you keep on looking to the future, you're going to miss today!

The plateau is exciting for two reasons. First, it provides the opportunity to move beyond the seemingly impossible. Second, once the plateau is surmounted, what preceded it takes its place in insignificance. The only issue of the plateau is endurance.

Steps to Becoming Reasonably Thin

- Endure!

Prayer

Father, incline my heart to endurance. Help me run the race to win. Keep me focused on today and only what will honor You. I'm determined to become reasonably thin because it honors You, because it brings You glory. I know You'll go there with me. I know that on the other side of endurance is wonderful treasure for me. Thank You. In the name of Jesus, amen.

25

Breaking Old Habits

You shall utterly destroy all the places where the nations which you shall dispossess served their gods, on the high mountains and on the hills and under every green tree. And you shall destroy their altars, break their sacred pillars, and burn their wooden images with fire; you shall cut down the carved images of their gods and destroy their names from that place.
—Deuteronomy 12:2–3

The Israelites were instructed to destroy the altars of the conquered nations so that they would not return to their habit of compromising and worshiping false gods. It was not enough that they would say they would not worship false gods. God wanted them to take preemptive action to eliminate the tendency toward the habit. We have to do the same thing with destructive habits.

I think we are all likely to have a habit or two. Perhaps it is the way we drive to work. Maybe it is the doughnuts we pick up along the way. A thought occurs to us. We act on it. It feels good. We do it again and again. There it is. Now it is a habit.

Habits can be either good or bad. But, either way, they

need to be evaluated from time to time. We are to be aware not only of what we are doing, but of why we are doing it. A part of the problem with a habit is that, if we do it often enough, it becomes somewhat automatic. It is as if we are once removed from the act. We do the same thing over and over as if we were not actually thinking about it. But we are thinking about it. It is just that the thought has faded into the background. That can be a problem.

> *The word* habit *is too general. A habit is made of component parts. You won't understand or change a habit easily without isolating and responding to each aspect of it.*

We all are responsible for our thoughts, behaviors, and the motivations behind them. When we develop habits, we tend to forget the motivation and the thoughts behind them. We simply do things because they were somehow satisfactory before. That is a problem for Christians. We are supposed to be sure that our thinking and behavior are consistent with what God wants. Habits can encourage us to forget. Let's look at Morgan and how her habit was affecting her life.

Morgan

"Why do you always have to have extra pancakes?" I asked Morgan.

"Because I've always done it that way," she said.

"What kind of reason is that?" I goaded her. "You do something over and over again just because you did it before? You cut your finger once. So you continue doing it because you've done it before?" We shared a few moments of laughter, then resumed our discussion.

> *When we develop habits, we tend to forget the motivation and the thoughts behind them. We simply do things because they were somehow satisfactory before. That is a problem for Christians. We are supposed to be sure that our thinking and behavior are consistent with what God wants.*

"That's the problem when we call something a habit," I explained. "The word *habit* is too general. A habit is made of component parts. You won't understand or change a habit easily without isolating and responding to each aspect of it." Those aspects or component parts of a habit are thoughts, behavior, feeling, and repetition. Let me show you how they work in my recommendations for Morgan.

Her first problem was in thinking that she wanted extra pancakes. If that is what she thinks, then that is more than likely what she will act on. I suggested that she change her thinking from wanting extra pancakes to wanting to develop relationships. It is not enough to stop the thinking that is in error. The erroneous or problematic thinking has to be replaced with the right thinking.

Then I suggested that she change her behavior to reflect her thinking. That would mean that instead of investing her energy in eating the extra pancakes, she would invest her energy in talking with people present at breakfast.

Finally, I told her that her feelings would follow her thoughts over time. Here's how it looked in practicality.

"The next time you have breakfast, don't make extra pancakes," I said. "Instead, plan to talk with your kids, and check up on how they're doing in school."

"So do I just sit there, and watch them eat?" she asked.

It is not enough to stop the thinking that is in error. The erroneous or problematic thinking has to be replaced with the right thinking.

"No," I said. "Sit there, and watch your children grow up. Listen to how they think. Listen to how they talk. Look into their eyes instead of looking at their plates. Let them know, by doing this, that you are interested in them. Trade in your pancakes for interest in your children and appropriate modeling for them."

"So what do I do if I'm out alone eating?" she asked.

"That's a good question, Morgan," I said. "It shows me that you are planning ahead. And that is one of the most important things to do to eliminate destructive eating."

"So what do I do?" she asked.

"Take stationery with you when you eat alone," I said. "In the place where you would have eaten those extra pancakes, instead invest in communication with friends or relatives. Show your appreciation in a note or letter. When you've finished writing to all of those you know, start all over again with the intent of edifying as many people as you can. Remember, it's always a good time to study the Word and invest in your spiritual growth. This isn't avoidance, it is getting a life."

Morgan followed my instructions, and in a short matter of time she became comfortable without her extra pancakes. Her habit disappeared, and her relationships became more fulfilling. As she is following the rest of the principles in this book, she, too, is moving closer to being reasonably thin. Let me go ahead and speak just a few necessary words on the subject of habits.

———

A habit is made up of thinking, feeling, behavior, and repetition. How do habits develop? Through repetition of the same thing over and over. How will you break habits related to eating? By repeating new thoughts, which will produce repeated new behaviors, and repeated new feelings, over time.

Steps to Becoming Reasonably Thin

- Review all eating behaviors, and isolate any eating habits.
- Eliminate any detrimental habits.
- Replace them with responsible thoughts, feelings, and behaviors.
- Repeat responsible thoughts, feelings, and behaviors.

Prayer

Father, may my eating behavior be so consistent in glorifying You that I eventually consider no other way to do it. Thank You for the joy there is in Your having given me choices, with which I can show my love for You. Please show me any detrimental habits I have developed over time, so that I may eliminate them. Help me develop proper habits. In the name of Jesus, amen.

26

Exercising for the Right Reason

Nevertheless the people refused to obey the voice of Samuel; and they said, "No, but we will have a king over us, that we also may be like all the nations, and that our king may judge us and go out before us and fight our battles."
—1 Samuel 8:19–20

When Israel demanded a king, they paired their hopes and dreams with the wrong person. They were God's people, different from the crowd, but they wanted to be like the other nations. They had God, but they wanted a king. When they placed their hopes in the wrong thing, they were disappointed. That is the inevitable result of inappropriate pairings.

It Happens in Marriage Too

One of the cardinal errors I have found in the thinking of married couples is that sex should be inexorably linked to good times only. Unfortunately, because of that thinking, when difficulties between the spouses arise, sex is one of the first things to go. "If we're not happy, then I don't want to make love!" But an intimate sexual relationship is one way to reaffirm commitment, and it may be most valuable when times are difficult.

> *When they placed their hopes in the wrong thing, they were disappointed. That is the inevitable result of inappropriate pairings.*

When sex and emotional comfort or emotional connection are too closely linked, they become dependent on one another. When one wanes, so will the other. If that occurs, the couple have lost not just one but two supportive methods of encouraging the relationship. They have also lost one of the attributes that could encourage the other. That is what happens when we fail to see things for their own intrinsic value and instead relate their value to something else. It makes one or both of them vulnerable to extinction. This can happen in many areas of our lives including areas related to food. Where I see this most is when exercise is paired with weight loss or destructive eating.

Exercise is a very important part of our lives. It is a healthy thing and can be a very pleasant thing. Some people exercise because they enjoy the feeling of exertion and the sense of accomplishment. They enjoy building and strengthening their bodies. It makes their minds clear and their lives longer. Some people exercise to keep their bodies from getting stiff and inflexible. All of these are wonderful reasons to exercise. But it is not always that way.

Some people exercise as their principal method of weight

control. That is a problem because it detracts from the act of exercise, places the focus of exercise back on weight control or food. In addition weight loss can become dependent on exercise. If exercise ceases then weight will again become an issue.

> *If we connect losing weight with exercise or using an exercise machine, losing weight then becomes dependent on exercising. When we make that connection, exercise carries more emotional pressure than it should, and that emotional overload carried by exercise means that we are less likely to exercise.*

Sophie is an example of the danger of deliberately pairing exercise with weight loss. Let's look at her story and the results of pairing exercise with weight loss.

Sophie

"My husband and I bought an exercise machine because I wanted to lose weight," Sophie said.

"So how did it go?" I asked.

"It just stands there in the corner and stares at me!" she replied. "I think I used it for about a week."

"Why did you quit?" I asked.

"I lost interest," Sophie said. "Now, my husband looks at it and then looks back at me, and I know what he is thinking."

"What's he thinking?" I asked.

"The same thing he says," Sophie replied. "'Look at all of that money we've wasted.' And he's right. Now I just feel more guilt, and more like I've failed."

Sophie's discouragement was compounded by attaching her desired weight loss to an exercise machine. That creates justification. If I don't like the machine, then the problem is the machine. Once again, the problem and the solution are somewhere outside of the person.

If we connect losing weight with exercise or using an exercise machine, losing weight then becomes dependent on exercising. When we make that connection, exercise carries more emotional pressure than it should, and that emotional overload carried by exercise means that we are less likely to exercise. When we exercise less, our weight builds, and we may blame it on the lack of exercise. We may even blame it on the exercise machine.

If we exercise as a method of weight control, our focus will be back on weight. If exercise does contribute to our losing weight, it can become dangerous if we overuse it. Think of someone who struggles with anorexia on the exercise machine.

If we overeat and exercise to eliminate the weight, and we are successful at taking the weight off, exercise can reinforce destructive eating. Then exercise becomes attached to something unpleasant—destructive eating. Once again, we may then be more hesitant to exercise. If exercise is successful in weight loss, we may feel more comfortable with destructive eating.

Exercise is very important in our lives. My intention here is not to diminish it, but rather to caution pairing exercise with destructive eating. Do not triangle exercise into the relationship you have with destructive eating! We should exercise reasonably, because it is the right thing to do, not because it is a tool to lose weight. Losing weight is a by-product of exercise. It should not be the goal.

Steps to Becoming Reasonably Thin

- See the problem not as a weight problem, but as destructive eating that results in a weight problem.
- Remember, do not use exercise to resolve destructive eating.
- Detach exercise from any weight-loss agenda.
- Allow exercise to be its own adventure without the goal of weight loss.

Prayer

Father, open up my mind and heart to exercising. Help me detach exercising from destructive eating. Teach me to enjoy it for its own sake. Help me remove any agenda from exercising other than exercising for health and enjoyment. In the name of Jesus, amen.

27

Seeing Yourself Accurately

For I say, through the grace given to me, to everyone who is among you, not to think of himself more highly than he ought to think, but to think soberly, as God has dealt to each one a measure of faith.

—Romans 12:3

My business, my life, and my ministry, in part, are helping people live lives that bring honor to God. They come to me with lives broken and torn apart, unable to know themselves. They hide behind their sin and justification. They are lost behind their pain. They have come to a place where they do not know who they are.

There is the successful man who has come to believe mistakenly that he is the sum of his successes. There is the abandoned wife who is devastated, thinking that since her husband left, nothing of her remains. There are the endless numbers of people who equate acceptance with personhood and disappear when a relationship ends. It is far easier than most people think for frail human beings to think of themselves as something that they are not.

It is a part of what I must do, to look beyond the defensive behaviors, the anger, the arrogance, or the expressed hopelessness to the person inside. An unfortunate miscalculation of who we are is a cornerstone of dysfunction in contemporary society.

One of the most important things in the Christian life is for the Christian to see himself or herself accurately. Certainly that requires that we see ourselves in Christ, as new creations in Him. But it also requires that we not see ourselves inaccurately, which happens often when it comes to eating destructively.

> *An unfortunate miscalculation of who we are is a cornerstone of dysfunction in contemporary society.*

There is a common inaccuracy in the thinking of many who struggle with destructive eating. It is an inaccuracy with which we may hold ourselves back from being all that we can be. It may also be very harmful to others and to relationships. Let me use Cassie to show you this common encumbrance.

Cassie

I heard Cassie say something during a session that echoes what I have heard so many women say. She had said the same words to her husband.

"If you can't accept my weight, you can't accept me," Cassie said. Her husband was left with very little stamina and few words to respond. This was obviously a battle they had fought before.

"I do accept you!" he objected. "I love you!"

"You don't accept me," Cassie insisted. "You hate my weight. I know you do!"

"Yes, I do," her husband responded. "But I do accept you. I do accept you! Why can't you see that?"

Telling the truth is the only way out.

"No, you don't!" Cassie insisted again. "If you don't accept my weight, you don't accept me!"

Cassie had herself and her husband locked into a dilemma from which there was only one escape. There were several problems brought about by Cassie's asserting that if her husband did not accept her weight, he was not accepting her.

Her husband genuinely hated her weight problem, because he thought it diminished her health. It also had a negative affect on their sex life. Her assertion placed him in a no-win situation. Should he have denied or hidden his true feelings? Should he have given up his true feelings to be with his wife?

If Cassie believed her assertion that her husband must either accept her current weight or not accept her at all, other problems would have resulted. Let's take a look at some of them and see if we can dismantle them.

Cassie might have been tempted to keep the weight on until her husband accepted her weight. Unfortunately, that would have resulted in Cassie's hurting herself and her husband in an attempt to control him. But Cassie's weight should not be dependent on any outside influence. And this method of trying to control someone else is wrong, first, because it is accomplished by doing something that is wrong—hurting Cassie and her husband. Second, it is wrong because, in general, we are not intended to control others.

> *It is possible for someone to accept you as a person and, at the same time, not accept your weight.*

Cassie might not have felt she could trust her husband if he said he accepted her weight. She might have felt manipulated, that he was saying he accepted her weight, just placating her, to get her to adjust her weight. She might then have felt that if she adjusted her weight, he still might not have accepted her. She might have seen his love as conditional.

Cassie might then become dependent on his attitude about her weight, as to whether or not she would change it. This would then become her justification for keeping her weight as it was. In part she could blame him.

In Cassie's case, issues of trust would eventually be turned into suspicion. From that, resentment was likely to develop on both the part of Cassie and her husband.

What is the way out of this quicksand? Telling the truth is the only way out. Here is the first essential truth: You are not your weight! Do not equate who you are with your weight! If you die, and your body decays as it will, will you cease to exist? No. You are your spirit and soul. Your body is the earthly tent where your soul lives.

Here is the second essential truth: It is possible for someone to accept you as a person and, at the same time, not accept your weight.

Cassie's husband was right. He did accept her and loved her dearly. But she could not hear him, because she confused his attitude about her weight with his attitude about her—Cassie, the person. Interestingly enough, Cassie was doing the same thing herself. She did not accept herself, because she did not accept her weight. And, she did not accept her husband unless he accepted her weight.

Steps to Becoming Reasonably Thin

- Do not confuse your self with your weight.
- You, the person inside, have control over your weight.

Prayer

Father, help me separate my self from my weight. My identity is to be in You, not in my weight. Help me accept myself and those who do not accept my weight. In the name of Jesus, amen.

28

Using Your Imagination Selectively

Therefore hear the parable of the sower.
—Matthew 13:18

Once, when I was young, someone told me that I could be anything I wanted to be. That is not the kind of thing to say to a kid with a fertile imagination and a tendency toward antagonism. "OK," I replied. "I want to be a frog." I do not remember that they ever encouraged me in that way again!

Imagination need not be seen as either good or bad. The issue is what you do with it. In the verse above, Jesus used a parable to create a mental image in the mind of His listeners. God created the power of imagination and wants to use it in man. But like all else, the power of imagination can be used in the right way or the wrong way.

Hitler imagined control of the world. Michael DeBackey

imagined an artificial heart. Disney imagined cartoons. Alexander the Great imagined the strategy of war. Inherent in the mechanism of the mind is the ability to conceive of things that as yet are not there. Imagination is the fluid of invention, and from it we may create and demonstrate that we were made in the image of God. But we can also use it to victimize ourselves.

We may dream of chocolate and by doing so create a desire so intense that we excuse our behavior in getting it. In our minds we may see ourselves as deprived and in doing so create justification for eating for comfort. We may see ourselves as beautiful tomorrow, without the work required today, and set ourselves up for failure and destructive eating.

> *Imagination need not be seen as either good or bad. The issue is what you do with it.*

Imagination can be destructive when used inappropriately in the area of eating. Let's look at how Tania got herself in trouble with her inappropriate use of her own imagination.

Tania

"That morning when we all got together, we all talked about where we would go for dinner. We decided on a steak place across town. Then we went on about the day." Tania went on. "I thought throughout the day about sitting at this restaurant, having a sizzling steak and a baked potato with sour cream, chives, and butter. I could almost smell it."

"And then?" I asked eagerly. "I'm halfway to the restaurant with the description you've given!"

"Well, it was weird." Tania went on. "On the way to the restaurant, we passed a Chinese restaurant, and everyone made a quick decision to change plans and go Chinese for the evening! That is everyone but me!" she said.

In subscribing to our imaginings, we can create a type of pull that draws us to food, or we can create a type of aversion that can encourage us to fear food. God would not have us use our imaginations to encourage destructive eating.

"What happened with you?" I asked.

"I got mad!" Tania said. "I actually got mad at them for changing their minds! I was so embarrassed about getting mad! I actually pouted when I didn't get my way."

Tania had experienced the power of imagination. Unlike her friends, she had invested, during the day, in imagining the food she would eat and the restaurant where she would have dinner. She had an emotional investment in her imaginings. Because of that, she was more invested in the plan, more invested in the experience, than her friends were. When her friends changed the plans, she felt disappointed and frustrated. Her heart was set on steak and baked potatoes.

It is not that our imagination takes hold of us. It is that we buy into what we imagine. In subscribing to our imaginings, we can create a type of pull that draws us to food, or we can create a type of aversion that can encourage us to fear food.

God would not have us use our imaginations to encourage destructive eating. Let me show you how powerful imagination can be.

Exercise

Become calm just for a moment, and then watch your emotional responses as you imagine the following scenarios. First imagine the scenario, then wait ten or fifteen seconds as you visualize it and allow the feelings to make themselves known. You may feel them in the pit of your stomach or in your chest.

Scenario 1

A huge, salivating grizzly bear is charging through the door, paws in the air, claws extended, tearing at the air, and he's coming after you!

———————[pause]———————

As you imagined the grizzly's approach, what were the feelings you experienced? List them below. You may have one. You may have had several.

I felt _____.
I felt _____.
I felt _____.

(Here are some examples: fear, anxiety, like I wanted to fight, like I wanted to run, terrified, etc.)

Let's try another scenario. Again, remain calm for a moment. Imagine the scenario, then pause for ten to fifteen seconds and wait for the feelings.

Scenario 2

Someone you love dearly and haven't seen for a terribly long time is walking through the door, and they're coming toward you to say "hello."

———————————[pause]———————————

As you imagined this person approaching, what were the feelings you experienced? List them below.

I felt _____.
I felt _____.
I felt _____.

(Here are some examples: excitement, sadness, tenderness, guilt, hurt, joy, etc.)

As you imagined the grizzly bear, you probably felt frightened and desperate to escape. Your heart may have beaten more rapidly, and there may have been an internal flush of anxiety and discomfort.

> *Your feelings were real even though your thoughts were false. If you want to control your feelings, especially those with which you drive yourself to eat or to not eat, make the right choices with your thoughts.*

When you imagined someone you love approaching, you may have felt a sense of pleasure, perhaps delight. If you had problems the last time you saw them, you may have felt more bittersweet feelings.

What is important here is that your feelings changed based solely on what you thought, solely on what you told yourself, solely on what you imagined. Your feelings responded to your thoughts. Your feelings were real even though your thoughts were false. If you want to control your feelings, especially those with which you drive yourself to eat or to not eat, make the right choices with your thoughts. You are in control. Your imagination cannot take you anywhere. You can take yourself places in your imagination. You are in control. Be sure that your imaginings honor God.

Steps to Becoming Reasonably Thin

- Accept responsibility for your imagination.
- Do not let your mind dwell on imaginings of food or hunger.
- Do not let your imagination linger on anything that would dishonor God.

Prayer

Father, I give my imagination to You. May my thoughts and imaginings be trained in this process to honor You. Please call it to my attention when my imaginings dishonor You, so that I may change my imaginings. In the name of Jesus, amen.

29

Using Words Selectively

So it was, when his master heard the words which his wife spoke to him, saying, "Your servant did to me after this manner," that his anger was aroused.

—Genesis 39:19

In the verse above, anger was aroused by an account given in words. The account, by the way, was not true. We get angry when we hear on the radio that some injustice has been done. We weren't there when the injustice was done. But the account, given in words, incites our anger. Words affect us. We hear that a friend has been honored for his good work. We are happy for him. The words that we heard about the event encouraged us to feel happiness. Words affect us.

There is great danger in, and there are quite possibly laws against, running into a crowded theater and shouting, "Fire! Fire!" Why? If there is no fire, then it is just a lie. So why would we be forbidden to do it? It is because words have an affect on us. It is because if we believe the words we will act on them.

Some words are very subtle in their impact on us. If I tell myself that I am a frog, the likelihood is that I will not begin to hop about as if I were shopping for a new lily pad. At least, I hope I would not. But if I say to myself that I am freezing, I might feel compelled to put a jacket on. Now, I am neither a frog nor am I freezing, but I will be more likely to act on one word than on the other. Why is that? It is because one is remote from any possibility while the other is simply unlikely.

Words—what we tell ourselves—stimulate us to some type of action. That is exactly why we must be careful about the words we use. This is especially true when it comes to dealing with destructive eating.

If I say I am fat when I am not, and I choose to believe that I am fat, I may react in an extreme fashion and choose to eat in a highly restrictive fashion. Since I am not fat, choosing to eat in a highly restrictive way could be life-threatening. Let's look at Charisse as an example of how words affect our eating behavior.

Charisse

"I feel so driven to eat!" said Charisse. "I can't stop myself!"

"Can you give me an example?" I asked.

"Yes," she said. "Just yesterday, I was leaving the library after doing some research for a few hours, and I was starving! But I had had breakfast only hours before! I just had to get home and eat! How could that happen?"

Charisse was experiencing something common to those who struggle with destructive eating. She was buckling under the power of her own words. Let's look at and evaluate the characteristics of the words she was using to drive herself.

"I was starving!" First of all, this was not true. It was a lie. Because it was extreme in nature, a survival response was prompted. Because she believed this lie, Charisse felt that she had to eat, that she had no reasonable option.

Words—what we tell ourselves— stimulate us to some type of action. That is exactly why we must be careful about the words we use. This is especially true when it comes to dealing with destructive eating.

"I can't stop myself!" Once again, this was not truth—also a lie. The use of the word *can't* made Charisse feel helpless and hopeless. And even though she was neither, she convinced herself with this lie that she might as well eat because the situation was hopeless.

"I just had to get home and eat!" Again, not true, but a lie. With this lie containing the word combination *had to*, Charisse created pressure on herself to eat. The pressure was all self-inflicted.

"How could that happen?" Here, by speaking in a passive frame of reference, Charisse led herself to believe that she had no responsibility in the matter. Because of that, she felt that she had no control.

Because of the use of these words and the feelings that they generated, Charisse would be likely to

1. shift into survival mode, which tends to lend itself to desperate actions, fueling anxiety;
2. feel driven to get relief, and justified in doing so;

3. feel helpless to do otherwise;
4. feel victimized by the process;
5. feel guilty about her behavior, without understanding her own responsibility for her thoughts;
6. feel vulnerable to the same thing happening again;
7. feel helpless about stopping a reoccurrence, because she does not know how it happened; and
8. feel hopeless about the situation, and the future, as it relates to this destructive eating.

How did Charisse resolve this situation? She questioned her words and the thinking behind them. Then she conformed her words and thinking to the truth. Here is how that looked in her journal as Charisse challenged her own words.

"I Was Starving!"

"Was I really starving? Was I about to die for lack of food? No. I was actually hungry. That would produce a feeling of discomfort, not a feeling of desperation. I can choose to use words that represent the truth and that will not produce desperation that prompts destructive eating behavior. I could have said that I was hungry."

"I Can't Stop Myself!"

"Is it true that I couldn't stop myself? No. I could have stopped myself. I could have chosen not to go home. I could have chosen not to eat. I could have chosen words that would have supported responsible behavior, instead of words that I used to drive myself."

"I Just Had to Get Home and Eat!"

"Is it true that I had to? No, I didn't have to. I chose to. I used pressure words that created a sense of pressure. I could have chosen other words. I could have said that I wanted to go home and eat. There would have been no desperation in those words, and I could have more easily decided not to eat."

"How Could That Happen?"

"This didn't just happen to me. I caused this to happen. If I caused it to happen, I can do it differently. I hold the power. I always have."

Here is how the situation would have been had Charisse selected words of truth. After being at the library for a few hours Charisse would have felt hungry. Knowing that she would eat at noon, she would have waited until then to eat. Perhaps she would have stopped at the water fountain to have some water to bring temporary relief from the slight discomfort of hunger. In following through until noon, Charisse would encourage her own responsibility in her thinking and behavior. Her sense of self-control and self-esteem would be enhanced, and her destructive eating would diminish. If she continued with this pattern of responsibility, over time her destructive eating would cease to exist. When her destructive eating ceased to exist, her weight problems would cease to exist. Charisse's did. Now she is reasonably thin. I wonder if Charisse's words would drive you.

Example

Let's try a scenario. Become calm for a moment. Say the words in the scenario to yourself, then pause for ten to fifteen seconds and wait for the feelings.

Scenario 1

"I'm starving!"
——————————[pause]——————————

As you thought to yourself that you were starving, what feelings made their presence known? List them below:

I felt _____.

I felt _____.

(Examples: desperation, fear, ill at ease, anxious, etc.)

Let's do another one. Remember, remain calm for a moment. Say the words in the scenario to yourself, then pause ten to fifteen seconds and wait for the feelings.

Scenario 2

"I want to eat!"

————————————[pause]————————————

As you thought to yourself that you wanted to eat, what feelings made their presence known? List them below:

I felt _____.

I felt _____.

(Examples: excitement, power, slight anxiety, etc.)

What is the difference in the feelings between saying that you are "starving" and saying that you "want to eat"? One statement produces a desperate feeling. The other does not.

To say that you are starving taxes your emotional system by placing a survival statement in the system. Adrenaline is released, and a fight-or-flight response is induced. At that point, the search for food takes on the air of urgency and desperation.

To say that you want to eat engenders a sense of responsibility and freedom to choose. The feeling that accompanies that sense of choosing is a feeling of well-being, and to assert what you want actually works to build self-esteem.

There is another question here. Is it true that you are "starving"? In most cases that will not be true, and like Eve, we will place ourselves under self-inflicted stress by telling ourselves a lie. If we tell ourselves the truth, we will not place ourselves in artificial, desperate straits. We will not drive ourselves to self-defeating and self-abusing behaviors, in this case overeating.

Steps to Becoming Reasonably Thin

- Be selective with your words, choosing on the side of truth and accuracy.

Prayer

Father, help me to speak accurately, so that I don't create my own unnecessary pressure. I want to live in truth and see myself accurately. Please draw my attention to my use of words that lead me into self-sabotage, so that with Your power I may change them. Please make me aware of the words I use that are acceptable to You, so that I may learn to repeat them. In the name of Jesus, amen.

30

Analyzing Your Own Statements

Let the words of my mouth and the meditation of
my heart
Be acceptable in Your sight,
O LORD, my strength and my Redeemer.
—Psalm 19:14

Can you imagine what impact Christians would have on the world if the words of all Christians honored God? What would it look like if all people in the world spoke in such a way that was acceptable to God? The impact would be phenomenal!

What we say to others and to ourselves has a powerful impact on our lives and the lives of others. Why is that? It is because words carry our thoughts and feelings.

Have you ever noticed how your words change the angrier you get? That is because our words are carriers of our feelings. That is one of the reasons why we feel relief when we talk about our troubled feelings with a friend or a counselor.

When we talk, we are getting our feelings out. When we talk, we are also getting our thoughts out.

Like freight cars of a train, words carry things. They are a delivery system that picks up something from one place and delivers it to another. They carry more than thoughts and feelings too. They also carry all of the other freight that those thoughts and feelings have picked up along the way.

When I hear the words of certain songs, I drift back to the time period when that song was popular. The words of the songs bring with them all of the memories and feelings from the past. A tender love song brings back different memories and feelings from those of a song about working for the railroad. Words do the same thing. They come with baggage attached.

When I hear the words of John F. Kennedy, "Ask not what your country can do for you; ask what you can do for your country," there are many feelings that flood to the brim of my consciousness. I feel the feelings of sadness at his death, the feelings of pride of being an American, and the feelings of pressure to contribute to my country.

> *Like freight cars of a train, words carry things. They are a delivery system that picks up something from one place and delivers it to another.*

When certain words are placed together, they combine to produce pressure. The words *to* and *have* become pressure words when they are placed together in a certain order. I feel that pressure when I say I "have to do" something. I feel a broader range of feeling when the word used is more all-inclusive. There is a different feeling when I say, "I feel bad today" from when I say, "I always feel bad."

A great deal of defeat can result from using the wrong words. Let me show you how this works with food. Janice is a great example.

Janice

Janice said that she had been doing quite well with her eating behavior until she went to visit her best friend back in Michigan.

"I was there for ten days and did just fine until the last night before I left. Then I binged."

I asked what she had eaten when she binged.

A great deal of defeat can result from using the wrong words.

"I went to the store and bought brownies, ice cream, and candy," she said. "I was real good on the airplane coming home, though. I just had to get back in control."

I showed Janice three things that her statements revealed: First of all, she had never been out of control. She had eaten brownies, ice cream, and candy. She was very selective in choosing these three foods. She was, in fact, very much in control.

Second, she brought pressure on herself by telling herself that she "had to" get back into control. The words *had to* when used together are pressure words that create anxiety.

And there was one more thing. Janice used the word *control*. When the word *control* is used by someone who struggles with destructive eating, the word itself may embody all past failures to "get control." It may bring those memories along with the word. So the word *control* actually brings with it a greater fear of defeat and hopelessness based on the past. It is an emotionally laden word. It is laden with the past, in this case, a negative past of failures.

I suggested to Janice that she refer to *choices*, instead of using the word *control*. Let me tell you why. The fact that Janice had done well for nine of the ten days she was away meant that she made nine days' worth of good choices. Using the word *choice* would separate out the good choices from the bad. *Control* tends to lump them all together, and because of that it tends to be seen as an absolute. Either I was in control (all of the time), or I wasn't. The end result would likely be negative, because there is no such thing as perfection in our behavior.

I suggested to Janice that she celebrate her success. First, her bingeing had vastly diminished since she started using the principles of *Reasonably Thin*. That is success. Second, all of those nine days when she made good decisions could have been nine days of bingeing.

I suggested that her celebration not involve food. It is important not to associate food with such things as self-reward.

The analysis of her words was taxing on Janice, but it was a part of what she chose to do to become reasonably thin. Let me show you how you can do the same thing.

How to Analyze Your Own Statements

Look for and eliminate unnecessary pressure words. Here are some pressure words: *have to, must, ought to, got to, should*. Replace these words with words that encourage personal responsibility and freedom of choice at the same time. Use words such as *want to, would like to, choose to*, etc. You will feel the pressure relieved as you change from pressure words to words that encourage personal choice.

> *Using the word* choice *would separate out the good choices from the bad.* Control *tends to lump them all together, and because of that it tends to be seen as an absolute. Either I was in control (all of the time), or I wasn't. The end result would likely be negative, because there is no such thing as perfection in our behavior.*

Look for and eliminate words that are extremes or that tend to include both the good and the bad together. Look for and eliminate words that are all-inclusive such as *all, every, nothing, everything, entire, never*. Replace them with more specific words such as *this time, this part, at times, occasionally*, etc.

Look for and celebrate overlooked successes. Try to find the best in yourself. What good choices did I make today? Did I choose not to think about food? Did I resist temptation? Did I eat on time?

Look to see if you are being realistic. Are there any attempts to be perfect? If you are not being realistic, change your thinking to reflecting reality. Remember, we cannot be perfect on this earth, but we should become mature.

Look for any lies. Replace them with the truth. Change "I was out of control," to "I did not eat on time at lunch." Change "I couldn't help myself!" to "I chose to eat at the wrong time at lunch." Change "I must be perfect" to "I am not happy with this one particular area of my eating behavior."

Look for and eliminate negative forecasting, and change it to the truth. Change "It will always be this way!" to "I know that God will empower me to live successfully in this area."

Remember that words are loaded with a great deal of history and bias. Be sure that the railroad car that delivers your words to you and to others is loaded with only the cargo you had planned. Be sure that there is no dangerous freight aboard.

Look for and eliminate negative thinking. Replace it with the whole truth, including both the positive and the negative. Replace "I look so bad today!" with "My weight bothers me, but even today I am working to change that."

Look for helpless thinking, and change it to responsible thinking. Change "I can't!" to "I won't!" Change "This situation is hopeless!" to "This situation is within my power to change."

Look for blaming and replace it with personal responsibility. Change "He's trying to sabotage me!" to "I'll do what is right, no matter what."

Remember that words are loaded with a great deal of history and bias. Be sure that the railroad car that delivers your words to you and to others is loaded with only the cargo you had planned. Be sure that there is no dangerous freight aboard.

Steps to Becoming Reasonably Thin

- Evaluate your statements, eliminating what will hold you back and including what encourages personal responsibility.

Prayer

Father, help me guard my thoughts against robbers of the truth. Keep me vigilant against words that lie to me and tell me I am helpless. Keep me vigilant against words that rob me of responsibility and success. In the name of Jesus, amen.

31

Talking and Listening to Yourself

But Jesus, knowing their thoughts, said, "Why do you think evil in your hearts?"
—Matthew 9:4

Almost every time I fill a glass with water, I run water over the top and have to clean it up. I have watched myself do it, and I have heard myself say, in my own mind, *Why do you do that, you silly beaver?* I have no idea why I do that, but I do have an idea that the Lord may prefer that I not talk to myself, about myself, in any derogatory way. By the way, I mean no disrespect to the beaver kingdom.

Only we and God know our private inner thoughts—the things we understand within ourselves, the things we say to ourselves. Imagine what it would be like if, all of a sudden, all of our private conversations within ourselves were put to voice, and everyone could hear them. Think about it for a moment. Would it change the way people see you? Would you want to change some of your inner conversations?

Why is it that what we say inside of our heads gets edited on the way out? Why aren't our inner thoughts consistent with our expressed thoughts? It is because when the thoughts are expressed, there may be instant accountability emanating from those who hear. When the words are kept within our heads, they often go unevaluated by us.

Since we act on our thoughts, it is important to bring them into some form of accountability. That includes the things we privately say to ourselves. Think about this verse for a moment. "But, speaking the truth in love, may [we] grow up in all things into Him who is the head—Christ" (Eph. 4:15).

Do you think that we should speak the truth in love to ourselves in the same way that we are to speak the truth in love *to others*? Do you think God would support a double standard in which we are one way in public, and then another way in private?

Let me show you how this relates to food, using Faith as an example.

Faith

I had Faith journal the negative things that she said to herself. She seemed hesitant to say what she was thinking out loud, so I thought journaling would be a safer method of disclosure for her. Why did I want to know what she was saying to herself? It was because, in session, she would frequently make faces that indicated that she was displeased with herself. I suspected that she had expectations of herself that were much too high and demanding. I would only know if this was true if she put her internal communication out in the open so we could analyze it. Here were some of her journal entries. Remember these are things she said to herself and about herself.

---

*D*o you think that we should speak the truth in love to ourselves in the same way that we are to speak the truth in love to others? Do you think God would support a double standard in which we are one way in public, and then another way in private?

Situation 1: Faith had eaten when she had not planned to. Here is what she said to herself: "You jerk. You know you shouldn't have done that!" "You're so useless!" "You're so pathetic!"

Situation 2: Faith succumbed to peer pressure and had eaten what and when she had not planned. "Why don't I just give up!" "I'm such an idiot!" "I'm such a fat pig!"

Situation 3: Faith had eaten in a reasonable way all day. "It's about time you got it right." "It took you long enough." "If it was so hard for you to get one day right, how can you possibly do a lifetime?"

What was Faith doing? Why would an intelligent person talk to herself in such a way? We can figure it out by asking these questions: What was the obvious end result of what she said to herself? And how did this internal communication help her achieve that result? Faith was using negative motivation to prompt herself to do better.

What were the more subtle, or unintended, side effects of using this type of communication? And how did this internal communication contribute to those side effects? If you look back over Faith's internal communication, you will find that it was self-demeaning, self-deprecating, self-critical, negative, fatalistic, cruel, and false. Think about it. Would you allow anyone to talk to you in this manner? I would hope not! But, like Faith, is this how you talk to yourself?

> *If you want to be reasonably thin, your internal communication must fall under your own accountability!*

Can you guess what emotional and psychological issues Faith struggled with? Can you guess what the side effects of this internal communication were? If you talk to yourself in this way, see if you relate. Her emotional and psychological side effects were low self-esteem, depression, and one more thing: Faith was an overachiever and a Christian. While she was miserable on the inside, she pretended to be all right on the outside. Because of that she was less than authentic.

All of these negative effects encouraged Faith to eat destructively. The negative motivation did not work for her. It worked against her. It stirred up anxiety and guilt. It encouraged her to think less of herself and to think that she was unworthy. That led to disappointment and a sense of futility in trying to control her eating at all.

Are you in the same predicament? I have known many Christians who were. There is a way out. If you want to be reasonably thin, your internal communication must fall under your own accountability! That is how Faith had to handle her situation. You can too. Here is how to fight against destructive internal communication and win.

Recognize that you are, in actuality, having conversations with yourself and that you are listening. Listen carefully to what you are saying. Conform your communication to the truth. Outlaw self-demeaning statements, such as "You stupid idiot!" or "You're so fat!" or "You're such a jerk." Outlaw fatalistic or self-limiting statements about the future: "You're never going to change" or "I'll never figure this out."

Use thoughts that encourage and nurture: "I ate at the right time, at noon" and "I'm on track to becoming reasonably thin!"

Steps to Becoming Reasonably Thin

- Remember when you talk to yourself that you are talking to a child of the King of kings, and He is listening.
- Talk to yourself in a way that would bring honor to God.
- Talk to yourself in a way that respects His creation.
- Ban all destructive communication from your thinking.

Prayer

Father, I am determined to speak to myself in a godly way. Please show me when I do otherwise, so that I can eliminate anything in my thinking that doesn't glorify You. Please bring to my attention when I speak to myself in a way that honors You, so that I may learn to repeat it. In the name of Jesus, amen.

32

Losing Obsessive Interest in Food

Casting down arguments and every high thing that exalts itself against the knowledge of God, bringing every thought into captivity to the obedience of Christ.

—2 Corinthians 10:5

I remember being in grade school, trying to listen to the teacher, but all I could think about was recess. I would sit at my desk and agonize as the clock above the door seemed to be in some sort of cruel time warp. I would think, *Hurry up, bell—ring! Right now, ring! I just know you're going to ring on the count of three: one, two, three. Now. Ring, bell! Ring now!!*

I could hear my teacher's muffled voice in the background as she read *Anne of Green Gables*. I would think to myself, *I don't care about* Anne of Green Gables*! Can't you see me turning blue? I need oxygen! I need out of here! Can't you see I'm going to die if I don't get out of here? I need to play!* I couldn't think of anything else but recess.

I would try to concentrate on the story that the teacher was reading to us, but I could see the playground from the window by my desk. I mentally counted the steps to the door through which I would go to recess. My desk was all neat and tidy so I could get away fast. I even had my sneakers aimed in the right direction, and I was on the edge of my seat. *Can't you see I'm having a nervous breakdown? Help! Please, bell, ring!* Fortunately recess came, though it was never long enough! And I was a mere vapor as I sped by the slower students to freedom beyond the hallowed halls and stuffy rooms of mundane book reports and stifling trivia, which to this very day I have not used!

Ending obsession requires two things. It requires the absence of the thoughts you do not want, and it requires the presence of the thoughts you do want. It takes both of these to end obsession. If you do not have them both, you are only postponing obsession, not getting rid of it.

Did you ever have a thought on your mind that seemed immune to your attempts to get rid of it? That was the struggle I was having before recess, and it was the struggle Clarisa was having in getting over her breakup with her boyfriend. Because Clarisa's obsessing was not about food, it might be easier for you to follow. You will not be distracted by comparing her story to yours. Unless, of course, you just broke up with your boyfriend! Take a look at her story, and then we'll look at how it applies to food.

Clarisa

Clarisa came to me ten months after she had broken up with her boyfriend. She couldn't stop thinking about him. According to Clarisa, her emotions were "running rough-shod" over her.

I asked how she had tried to stop thinking about him.

"I tell myself to stop thinking about him, that it was actually a good thing that we broke up. I try to think of all of the crummy things that he said to me. I tell myself it's over, that I'll find someone else. I even pray about him!"

Look closely, and you will see that all of her thoughts concerned themselves with her boyfriend! Her attempts to stop thinking about him all drew her back to the subject!

Clarisa thought that her emotions were driving her constant thoughts about her boyfriend. In actuality, Clarisa was prompting obsessive thinking about him in three different ways: First, she was thinking about him directly (direct obsession). She was also thinking about him indirectly and thinking about things related to him (indirect obsession). On the opposite side of the coin, there was something that Clarisa did not do. She did not redirect her thoughts elsewhere.

Ending obsession requires two things. It requires the absence of the thoughts you do not want, and it requires the presence of the thoughts you do want. It takes both of these to end obsession. If you do not have them both, you are only postponing obsession, not getting rid of it. In Clarisa's case, she had two problems. She not only thought about what she did not want to think about—her ex-boyfriend—but she also failed to redirect her thoughts elsewhere.

If you are thinking about food when you do not want to, or if you are thinking too much of the time about food, consider the possibility that you are obsessing on food. It is important to know that most obsession is a matter of choice.

How does obsession relate to food and how do we eliminate it? Here is the first half of the solution to obsessing on
food.

Control your thoughts. Recognize that you are thinking too
much of the time about food, or thinking about food when
you do not want to.

*Check to see if you are fighting against thoughts about food with
thoughts about food.* Here is an example of thinking that leads
to direct obsession: "I've got to stop thinking about food!" It
is a direct obsession because you are thinking directly about
food. You are actually using the word *food*. That will
inevitably draw your attention to food. That is exactly what
you do not want!

> *Let God's Word and His plan become
> more real to you than food! How can
> you do that? Invest the time and
> energy that you used to invest in food
> and in fighting your problem with
> eating, instead in learning more of
> Him. Invest it in obeying Him.*

Now here are two examples of thoughts that can lead to
indirect obsession: "I've just got to cut down [on eating]
tomorrow" and "This [destructive eating] has to end." Here
you are not using the word *food*, but the understood subject
is food. Once again, that will draw your thinking back to
food. And, again, that is exactly what you do not want!

Give up the battle against food! Instead, learn to redirect your
thoughts. In those places where you were thinking about
food or fighting thoughts of food, deliberately think about

something else not related to food. Here is something to remember: You cannot think two things at the exact same time! You can alternate between thoughts. But you cannot think two different thoughts at the exact same time. If you think you can, please call me for some serious therapy! If you are thinking about a conversation, you cannot be thinking of food at the same time.

When you become aware of thinking of food, shout internally, *"Stop!"* And then divert your thoughts elsewhere. When you do this, you are not fighting thoughts of food; you are stopping your thinking process. At that point, redirect your thoughts.

Get a life! Use the energy you used to use in obsessing about food in some constructive way. Distract yourself with something that is good for you and good for others.

Do not just try to change a habit. Recognize that God has changed your life. He has given you a new life, with new hungers. Acquaint yourself with your new hungers. "Blessed are those who hunger and thirst for righteousness, / For they shall be filled" (Matt. 5:6).

Let God's Word and His plan become more real to you than food! How can you do that? Invest the time and energy that you used to invest in food and in fighting your problem with eating, instead in learning more of Him. Invest it in obeying Him.

Does that sound boring to you? If it does, let that be an indicator to you of how your energy and emotions have been misdirected elsewhere. Your concentration on food has imbued food with the interest that belongs elsewhere. It has made food loom larger than life to you. It has made food take on significance that it should not have. This is misplaced interest and excitement. It is placed in an area that will not satisfy, and because of that, it will drain you instead of energize you. Not so with the Christian life.

There is nothing more exciting than the Christian life. If you have diverted your interest and excitement away from the Christian life and into food, you will rob yourself of the genuine joy and excitement that belong to every Christian.

Now let's add this to what you already know about predetermining a structure to your eating, and see how that relates to obsession. It is the second half of the solution to obsessive interest in food.

Predetermine your behavior. The purpose of determining to eat three times a day has everything to do with obsessing on food. You would think it would actually cause obsession to schedule three times a day to eat, but it does just the opposite. It limits, and most of the time eliminates, obsession.

Obsessing on food occurs when we think about food. Obsession is intensified when the decision-making process gets involved. Imagine walking through the mall and seeing the many things to eat. You can be making decisions right and left about what to eat and what not to eat! All of that time you are thinking about food. But, if you know you are going to eat at one o'clock or six o'clock, that is the instant answer to all of the questions. Eventually, by knowing that you are going to eat at a certain time, you will find yourself not even considering the question of whether or not to eat. At that point, all of the obsession caused by contemplating the questions will disappear.

Also, knowing you are planning to eat at specific times gives you an automatic answer to any request that you do otherwise! If someone asks you to stop by for a bite, you have your response already prepared. "Thanks for the invitation, but I'm planning on eating at six o'clock. I'd be happy to drop by and chat, though."

Eventually, these responses will relieve us of having to think about food much at all. The structure will give us assurance that we will be eating, so there is no need to give in inappropriately to hunger. At this point we will start to have our lives back. Let me add just a bit more encouragement here on how we communicate about our eating structure.

It is a better plan to say, "No, I want to eat at six o'clock at home, as I have a very nice meal planned" than to say, "No, I can't eat right now." In one, you are looking forward to something good and healthy. In the other you are trying not to do something unhealthy. One is positive; the other is negative. One is assertive; the other is helpless. One is responsible; the other is not.

This structure to eating also has another advantage. Some who struggle with destructive eating feel that friends or spouses, secretly or subconsciously, sabotage their attempts at healthy eating. The eating structure I have proposed will eliminate the necessity of seeing anyone as a saboteur. With the eating structure in place, you know exactly how you will eat. You have responses to any other suggestion already prepared. You can now eat reasonably, no matter what anyone else says.

Steps to Becoming Reasonably Thin

- Never allow obsession to live one moment longer than it takes to dismantle it!
- When it comes to food, fight for what is right rather than against what is wrong.
- Assume an attitude of victory!

Prayer

Father, I withdraw my permission to allow myself to obsess. Please help me as I learn to redirect my thoughts. Show me other interests in life that You would have me consider. I pray for Your support and power as I learn to say no when I'm asked to eat at times other than those that I have predetermined. Keep my heart on the structure of eating at three specific times, so that I can live unencumbered by unnecessary questions that lead to obsession and destructive eating. In the name of Jesus, amen.

33

Meeting Needs and Desires Legitimately

Jesus answered and said to her, "Whoever drinks of this water will thirst again, but whoever drinks of the water that I shall give him will never thirst."

—John 4:13–14

Jesus knew the real need of the Samaritan woman. She needed His life, His grace. To accept something else would have kept her coming back to the well that never provides lasting satisfaction. This verse demonstrates that legitimate needs and wants are to be met in legitimate ways.

Legitimate *relationship* needs or desires should be met through the development of relationships with people and through spiritual truths, not through a relationship with food. If you are lonely because you do not have the specific relationship you want, develop other relationships. As a Christian, remember the promise that you are never alone, and act on it. Do not turn to food.

Legitimate *psychological* needs or desires should be met psychologically, not with food. If confusion is plaguing you, seek clarity instead of wondering in turmoil and turning to food. God is not the author of confusion, so ask Him to reveal the truth to you. Until He does, do not keep on wondering. Trust that He will show you the way out of your confusion.

Legitimate *emotional* needs or desires should be met through emotional development, not with food. If you are anxious, see a physician for any possible physical contributors. If you cannot conquer it on your own, talk to a friend or see a counselor. Determine what might be contributing to the anxiety. Work through any underlying emotional issues to resolve the anxiety, but do not turn to food. God would not have you anxious. He says to turn to Him and give these cares to Him, because He cares for you. Do that, but do not turn to food.

Legitimate *spiritual* needs or desires should be met through the development of spiritual life, not with food. Every Christian has the desire to know and please the Lord. If you are out of touch with Him because of sin or neglect, there will be emotional discomfort. That discomfort is due to a strained relationship with the Lord. Turn to Him in prayer and obedience. Turn to the Bible to know Him better. Turn to Christian friends for fellowship and support, but do not turn to food. Take a look at how Mattie was trying to satisfy desires in the wrong way.

Mattie

"Sometimes I get angry, and sometimes I'm sad." Mattie was telling me about her relationship with her son. "I worry about him and the path he's on. He doesn't want anything to do with God."

My heart always has a strong current of hope when I hear

such stories. I know my mother felt the same way about me when I turned my back on God. The hope comes in knowing that if God turned me around, He can turn others around.

"What do you do with your worry and your anger?" I asked Mattie.

When eating is a substitute for resolving issues, the number of unresolved issues may compound the extent of the destructive eating.

"I don't know," she said. "I guess I just stuff it. I've gained thirty pounds since he started downhill."

"Does your son know how you feel about his destructive decisions?" I asked.

"I'm not sure. I try not to say anything. I just pray," Mattie said.

"Who are you talking to about this?" I asked. "Are there friends you can confide in?"

"No," she said. "My husband doesn't want me to tell anyone. He is very bitter about what has happened. I don't want to upset my husband because he gets so angry. I just don't want to rock the boat any more than it has already been rocked by my son."

"Have you talked to your husband about all of this?" I asked.

"Only a little bit," she said. "We don't talk much about anything."

"Why is that?" I asked.

"We just never have talked much. I used to talk easily, but my husband doesn't say very much, and I guess I've just gotten used to it." Mattie offered a bit more. "We used to talk more when we were dating, but not now."

Mattie was hurting, and she was lonely for communication with her husband. Her way of nurturing herself was to eat. Somehow that soothed the gnawing in her stomach. Her desire was not for food. It was for the welfare of her son. It was for a closer and more involved relationship with her husband. What she wanted was legitimate; it was righteous. But the way she was going about trying to satisfy that desire was wrong. She was using a physical means of trying to satisfy an emotional and psychological desire. Because of that approach, she was overeating and gaining weight. The original issues remained unresolved and were actually getting worse. Now her weight was also a problem.

How did Mattie eliminate her destructive eating? She did it, in part, by learning to follow the principles of *Reasonably Thin*, about not eating when she had not planned to or what she had not planned to eat. But the other part was about resolving the unresolved issues. Let me see if I can put it in a way that will work for you as well. Here are the steps to follow for meeting real needs or desires in the right way. I will use Mattie as the example.

---

*R*esolution *may mean that you have done all that you can do in the situation, no matter what anyone else thinks or does. You can be all right even if others are not all right with you.*

Step One: Identify the destructive eating and understand why it is a problem. For Mattie it was eating for the wrong reaons.

When eating is a substitute for resolution, the underlying issue remains unresolved, it grows, and a second issue, destructive eating, is created.

Step Two: Identify the unresolved or underlying issues. What were the wrong reasons for which Mattie was eating? She ate to nurture herself in the absence of enough nurturing from her husband, her son, and friends. She ate because she could not or would not talk with others, including her husband, about her problems. She ate because it calmed her anxious stomach and distracted her from her worries about her son.

When eating is a substitute for resolving issues, the number of unresolved issues may compound the extent of the destructive eating. Mattie had four reasons to eat: mood altering, isolation, comfort, and distraction. If she ate in regard to all of the issues, you can see how her weight would increase significantly.

Step Three: Use the time devoted to destructive eating on resolving the underlying issues instead. When you do this, you reverse the process, substituting resolution for destructive eating.

Instead of eating, Mattie began to seek resolution on her unresolved issues. She talked with her husband about getting some help (therapy) with their learning how to communicate better. He refused. The same thing occurred with her son. So I helped her to learn how to communicate with them, no matter what their responses were. At least she was talking about how she felt, instead of stuffing her feelings.

One of the main things she came to understand was that resolution does not always mean that relationship is restored, or that everyone is happy. Resolution may mean that you have done all that you can do in the situation, no matter what anyone else thinks or does. You can be all right even if others are not all right with you.

Mattie and I also spent time on her issue with worry. We looked to Scripture for how she was to handle worry, and she chose the scriptural path, giving God her anxieties. In the process, her faith was strengthened instead of her emotions being drained.

Mattie also explained to her husband that it would be healthy and helpful for her to talk to others about her problems with her son. They agreed on two people that they both trusted to keep confidences, and she began to talk with them, sharing her feelings there.

Mattie's dependence on food for comfort began to diminish as she experienced more emotional connectedness with friends and, to some degree, her family. She no longer eats as a source of comfort or as a substitute for relationship. By meeting legitimate needs and desires in legitimate ways, Mattie now lives reasonably thin.

Steps to Becoming Reasonably Thin

- Meet legitimate needs or desires legitimately.

Prayer

Father, You satisfy my needs even when You satisfy them through others. Please show me the legitimate needs and desires that I am trying to satisfy with food. Help me to meet those needs and desires legitimately. In the name of Jesus, amen.

34

Resolving Unfinished Business

If it is possible, as much as depends on you, live peaceably with all men.

—Romans 12:18

I had a client, Carol, who was raised on a horse ranch. When she was seventeen she was thrown by a horse and seriously injured. After recovering from her injuries, she was reluctant to get back on a horse. In fact, she had begun to be fearful of horses in general.

When Carol married at age nineteen she and her husband moved into a new home that had been prepared for them on the ranch. But her fear of horses persisted. It became so serious that she and her husband had to leave the ranch to get away from the horses. Over time Carol and her husband visited the ranch less and less. When grandchildren came along, Carol did not want to take them to the ranch. She wanted to keep them at home, which she saw as a safe haven.

Carol came to me with her husband, parents, and children. Her parents and her husband were seriously concerned about how Carol was withdrawing from them. They were also concerned that the children were becoming reclusive. What had happened was that Carol had never resolved her unfinished business regarding her riding accident. Because of that she was beginning to rob herself of her future. She was using her home away from the ranch as an illegitimate means of dealing with unfinished business. Because of that unfinished business, she came to therapy.

> *I do not think it is right to blame the past for our current thinking or behavior. But I do think it is right to acknowledge the impact the past has had on our lives, and then determine to deal responsibly today with that impact.*

I worked with Carol, helping her adjust to being around horses again. Eventually she was able to move back onto the ranch. Once she did, her children had the privilege of living the same type of wonderful childhood she had had. Carol's problem with horses is not unlike the unfinished business people have with one another.

Some of the greatest harm done in lives and relationships is the result of failing to resolve our pasts. That is true especially with our past hurts. I think about it as unfinished business. It is unfinished because the effects of the past still continue. I do not think it is right to blame the past for our current thinking or behavior. But I do think it is right to acknowledge the impact the past has had on our lives, and then determine to deal responsibly today with that impact.

Here is something to remember if you have been hurt in the past: You cannot change the past, but you can change its effects on you.

I have frequently encountered unfinished business in the lives of those who have struggled with destructive eating. It is not always the case, but I have found it to be frequent and significant. Let me show you how unfinished business preys on food, with destructive and sometimes lifelong consequences. Stacey is a good example.

Stacey

Stacey was a victim of abuse as a child. She was molested by a neighborhood boy when she was ten years old and he was sixteen. Stacey, like so many others who have been abused as children, grew up feeling bad about herself. Somehow, she did not think that what happened was her fault, but she blamed herself for not screaming or telling someone. She was afraid to tell her parents, not because she feared their reaction, but because she was afraid to let them down. And she was afraid of getting the boy in trouble.

Over the years, Stacey used food to comfort herself, to punish herself, and to protect herself. She surrounded herself with a visible wall of fat. She intended to be unacceptable to men. She intended to keep them at a distance, because she did not feel OK enough with herself to be in relationship with someone. She used her weight to keep herself from being hurt by someone she might care for. If they could not get close to her or did not want to get close to her, she would never have to deal with all of her fears and insecurities.

Stacey was using food for the wrong reasons: protection, comfort, and punishment. If food is used to avoid resolving unfinished business, a dependency on food develops. Eating becomes problematic, and unresolved issues from the past remain unresolved. If unresolved issues from the past remain the justification for destructive eating behavior, the pattern will persist, because the unfinished business will remain unfinished. At that point, resolving unfinished business becomes something to avoid, because it provides the justification for destructive eating. The cycle is now circular, and, without taking action to stop it, it will be endless. Here is something to remember if you have been hurt in the past: You cannot change the past, but you can change its effects on you.

Stacey had to look closely at her painful experiences from the past and evaluate the effects on her thoughts, feelings, and behavior. Stacey was launching a preemptive strike against men. She was giving them a reason to reject her, so that she would not get involved in a relationship and then be rejected. She did not want to get hurt anymore.

What Stacey was doing was equating relationship with pain. The fact is that relationship does not equate with pain, but all relationships have potential pain in them. Stacey had to learn to accept some pain as a reasonable part of a relationship between two people with sin natures. She learned to detach her past pain from current relationships by adjusting her expectations about current relationships.

Stacey was overprotected because of irrational fear, and she did not know how to protect herself properly. She learned how by developing reasonable boundaries and learning to trust her own instincts. She also learned that God is there and that she can rely on Him.

Once the purpose of the unfinished business was eliminated (the desire to protect herself inappropriately), and with following through with *Reasonably Thin*, her dependency on food diminished and eventually disappeared. The dependency was, in fact, transferred to her relationship to the Lord, as He guided her through resolving her unfinished business.

How to Detach Food from Unfinished Business

What were the steps followed to detach food from unfinished business? I will outline them for you here.

- *Recognize that you are eating for the wrong reasons.* How will you know if you are eating for the wrong reasons? If you are eating too little or too much, you are eating, or not eating, for the wrong reasons.
- *Determine what the underlying reason is.* In this case it was unfinished business from the past.
- *Detach the eating behavior from the unfinished business.* You do that by seeing them as separate from one another.
- *Eat according to the principles of* Reasonably Thin.
- *Resolve the unfinished business separately.*

Steps to Becoming Reasonably Thin

- Never let unfinished business be justification for eating in a destructive way.

Prayer

Father, I relinquish using my past as a justification for my destructive eating. Please take me through any unfinished business to get it resolved. I'm listening, Father. I commit to You to remain alert to those issues behind my eating destructively. In the name of Jesus, amen.

35

Living Confidently and Powerfully

Let your light so shine before men, that they may see your good works and glorify your Father in heaven.

—Matthew 5:16

I remember being in a volleyball tournament, and our team was on the sidelines in a huddle. It was a critical point in the tournament. Looking out over the huddle, I saw the other team line up to play, with their strongest server approaching the serve line.

"Oh, no!" I said. I had not planned to say it out loud, but I did, and my teammates heard me. They, in turn, looked at the court and saw the power server in her position. Immediately some of the other members of our team began to express alarm over this person being the next server. Our coach had to calm us down.

If I had said nothing, the panic would not have spread. I could have hidden it, and our team would not have been disrupted. I did not intend to have that type of impact on our team, but I did start the panic. I understood from that experience more of how my behavior could impact others. From that point on I determined to choose the right impact I was going to have on the team.

The first step in living confidently and powerfully is to determine what impact you want to have on this world. Let's start by understanding that we all have an impact on the world around us. We have no choice about whether or not we will have an impact on others, but we do have a choice about the type of impact we will have. How do we have an impact on others? We may have an impact directly or indirectly. Let me put that in the context of destructive eating.

Our direct impact comes from what we say and do to or for others. If a parent overfeeds a child, or a friend always encourages her friend to eat when they are out, there is direct impact.

Indirect impact occurs in several ways, first, through modeling behaviors that are then learned by others. It also occurs when the eating behavior of one person, and the results of that eating behavior, becomes so dominant or destructive that it robs others of that person's life or time.

> *We have no choice about whether or not we will have an impact on others, but we do have a choice about the type of impact we will have.*

What is the impact you have been having on others? You would not be reading this book if you were not interested in having a good impact on yourself and on others. Perhaps in the area of eating your impact has not been what you have wanted it to be. Then take heart. Part of what is so thrilling about *Reasonably Thin* is that the principles will help you understand how to make the right impact.

How do we live confidently and powerfully? First, choose the right impact you want to make. Second, do not do anything that you cannot do in faith, expecting God to bless it.

The first thing to do is to evaluate the current impact you are having in the area of food. How do we do that? Try answering these questions: In the area of food, what have I modeled for anyone who might have been watching me? In the area of food, what have I directly encouraged others to do? Let me give you an example in Blake.

Blake

Blake is an excellent speaker. I do not say that of too many speakers. Blake, however, is exceptional. Those who hear him on tape are drawn to God's truth through him. His thinking is clear, and his words are effective. Listening to him leaves people inspired and wanting more. But there was a problem.

Blake was significantly overweight. Some who heard him speak in person discounted what he said because of his weight. He was angry at their shallow perception of him. I agreed that it was unfortunate that people look at destructive eating with condemnation. But there was the temptation for

Blake to blame others for what was his problem. The fact was that people had difficulty hearing him, in part, because he had a problem with eating. He had to learn to be careful to look to his own responsibility, and not to the responsibility of others.

As a Christian and a speaker, Blake was modeling that destructive eating was OK. But it is not. Those of us who teach and speak are held to higher standards. I believe it is because when we do something, we sanction it in the eyes of others. Blake was demonstrating that obedience in all areas of your life is not necessary for success. That is true, but should we not model that obedience should be thorough and complete? What is the impact we want to have as Christians? For the Christian, it is one thing: to let the light of Christ shine through us in such a way that He is seen and God our Father is glorified.

Once we have determined that this is the impact we choose to make, we are farther along the way to becoming and remaining reasonably thin. Why is our choice of impact so important in living confidently and powerfully? Because when we decide to live for the cause of Christ, it is then that we may attach ourselves to His indwelling power.

Let's talk more about living confidently and powerfully. This next verse is very important in that regard. It is from the pen of Paul in his letter to the Romans: "But he who doubts is condemned if he eats, because he does not eat from faith; for whatever is not from faith is sin" (Rom. 14:23).

How do we live confidently and powerfully? First, choose the right impact you want to make. Second, do not do anything that you cannot do in faith, expecting God to bless it.

How do you do something in faith? If what you are doing is consistent with what God's Word says, and you do it looking to Him for the power to do it, you are doing it in faith. You have faith in Him, and because of that, you do what He says. That is life in faith. God can bless that. He can put His power behind every act of faith.

If God can bless what you are doing, it will also bring Him glory. If it brings Him glory, He is pleased. Life cannot be any more exciting than to live a life in faith that you expect God to bless, and that brings Him glory! To do that, wherever He has called you, is the definition of our highest and best! How does that apply to eating? The questions below will serve as a guideline for you.

God will certainly bring eventual good out of things that we do, because He promises to. In these questions, though, when I ask if God can bless this something, I mean can you expect that He would bless the specific act described. Here is the list of questions.

Can I, in Faith, . . . ?

—— *Can I, in faith, overeat and compromise my health and expect God to bless that? Or can I, in faith, undereat and compromise my health and expect God to bless that?* No. Our bodies are God's. For Christians, they are temples where He dwells. Certainly we cannot expect that God would bless our mistreatment of His creation. Also, as Christians we are to represent Him on this earth. He will certainly not bless our treating our bodies in such a way that would cut our time short on this earth.

—— *Can I, in faith, eat when I had not planned to, if it has a negative impact on my health, and expect God to bless that?* When we determine to eat in a healthy way, at certain times of the day, eating at additional times over a period of time can be harmful to your health. God will not bless that perpetual overeating.

—— *Can I, in faith, eat as a way of dealing with my emotional distress and expect God to bless that?* No. When we eat to resolve our emotional distress, we are using an illegitimate means of resolving a legitimate issue. This leaves the problem unresolved and creates problems related to food. God will not bless that, so it cannot be done in faith.

— *Can I, in faith, eat to protect myself from intimacy, rather than having proper boundaries, and expect God to bless that?* No. Once again, this is a use of an illegitimate means of satisfying a legitimate desire for proper boundaries. Again, the original issue is not resolved, and new destructive issues with food are created.

— *Can I, in faith, eat to punish someone else or myself and expect God to bless that?* No. The objective here would be to explore why you would desire to punish anyone and resolve the issues that led you there. God will not bless eating as a form of punishment. Nor will He bless not eating when it is used as a form of punishment.

— *Can I, in faith, eat destructively, modeling that to others, and expect God to bless that?* No. God cares what you model for others, and He would have you model what is right. He will not bless your destructive modeling. You cannot model destructive eating behavior and rightfully expect God to bless it. You cannot do it in faith.

If these things cannot be done in faith, are they sin? Yes. Do you treat things differently if they are sins from the way you treat them if they are just problems? If they are sin, we must confess, repent, comply, and continue. If they are things done in faith, God will honor them and empower us! Take a look at the other side of the coin.

— *Can I, in faith, eat in a structured way that keeps me from eating destructively and expect God to bless that?* Yes. When you determine to eat at predetermined times during the day and determine to eat predetermined foods, all of which are healthy, God will bless that. Determining to have that structure relieves you of obsessions with food, and God will bless that.

—   *Can I, in faith, graciously decline to eat at times when I had not planned to and expect God to bless that?* Yes. As long as this is done with loving-kindness.

More on Living Confidently and Powerfully

The third thing to do in order to live confidently and powerfully is to have realistic expectations. Expect progress, not perfection.

Fourth, to live confidently and powerfully, allow God to teach you from your failures. God uses our failures to teach us. They are great places for us to grow. The fact is, no matter what we are experiencing, God can turn it to our good through faith in Him. Even if God cannot bless an exact behavior that is wrong, He does promise to bring eventual good for the Christian.

Fifth, until you have developed comfortable discipline, just do better each day than the day before. Let this be your guide. On this earth the gauge for how well you are doing is progress, not perfection.

Steps to Becoming Reasonably Thin

- Determine to eat in a way that can be done in faith, knowing that God will bless it.
- Do it no other way!

Prayer

Father, I recognize that this area is no less important than every area of this life that belongs to You. May I never diminish Your power in any area of my life. In the name of Jesus, amen.

36

Experiencing
the Thrill of Victory

My brethren, count it all joy when you fall into
various trials, knowing that the testing of your
faith produces patience. But let patience have its
perfect work, that you may be perfect and
complete, lacking nothing.

—James 1:2–4

When I was a young girl, I developed a huge crush on a boy who was much older than I was. I was friends with his sister, and in the endless hours I spent at her house, I hoped I would encounter him. Finally, it happened. The object of my affection and two of his friends were going ice-skating. Either to be polite or in response to the intense longing that permeated my entire being, he asked if his sister and I wanted to come along.

"Oh, yes!" I said, once I could breathe. "But, I don't have any skates!"

"I've got an extra pair upstairs you can use if you'd like," he said.

"Great!" I chirped.

"Good, then," he said. "We'll meet you guys over there."

"Swell!" I said. (We used words like *swell* back then.)

My friend and I entered reverently the hallowed halls of my heartthrob's closet, and there were his ice skates, in a sacred corner atop other discarded footwear.

> *This is not some small irritant that nags at our lives and hampers us from getting to the big things other people get to deal with. This is the big thing; this is the trial.*

I was so thrilled at the opportunity that I failed to notice until we got to the frozen lake that the skates seemed at least five times larger than my foot size. And they were hockey skates, not figure skates. My world was crumbling before my eyes! The man of my dreams and his big feet were about to skate out of my life without me!

"No way!" said my inner champion. And with that I laced on the skates and stood upright, like any self-respecting biped. It was then, and wisely so, that I gave immediate and serious consideration to the fact that I did not know how to ice-skate.

Aha! I thought, ever the clever one. *No one else knows I don't know how to skate!*

I managed to stand quite erect for hours and say repeatedly, "No, thanks. I think I'd rather just watch a while."

Originally, what I wanted to do was win the affections of my heart's target. But in struggling to stay on the skates and on the ice, I began to enjoy the slight movement on the ice. I later returned frequently with the right size figure skates.

In the long run, I developed a serious fondness for ice-skating that warms my heart today just to think of it. Out of this seemingly insignificant struggle came one of the finest pleasures of my life. There, I learned that I could rise to the occasion when it became necessary. I also learned to look at the size of the skates before you say you'll wear them!

For some of us, until we eliminate it, destructive eating will be our struggle, our trial. Our faith will be tested in the area of food. This is exactly where our character will be developed. This is exactly where we are to reap the by-products of obedience. This is not some small irritant that nags at our lives and hampers us from getting to the big things other people get to deal with. This *is* the big thing; this is the trial. Certainly we will have more, but this is the one we are allowed to face, at this point, to test our faith. Do not look beyond it to some seemingly more noble venture. This destructive eating or the temptation to eat destructively is exactly where your faith is to be developed. This is God's plan.

What are the by-products of facing this challenge and conquering it? What are the by-products of glorifying God in the area of our eating? Being reasonably thin. And what else? Spiritual growth. Emotional stability and maturity. Psychological stability and maturity. Comfort around others. Relationships healed. Diminishing of and eventual absence of unnecessary fear, anxiety, worry, and insecurity. Use the trial of food to thoroughly reap all of the benefits of obedience. Let me show you with Corina what is possible with you.

Corina

"I've been experiencing the thrill of victory you talked about. It's wonderful!" Corina said. "I never would have thought that the spiritual, emotional, and psychological growth and maturity I longed for could actually be generated by dealing with my destructive eating. But it's true. I kept wanting to grow spiritually, as if it were a separate area of my life from that of my eating behavior. I kept avoiding the area of my destructive eating and trying to move on to something deeper, or better, to work with. But it was the problem with food that held all of the secrets of growth for me. Now I thank God for the problems I used to have with food. Dealing with them has taken me where I always wanted to go. I didn't need to look for something else. It was right in front of me all of the time."

I asked Corina to take me through the process and show me how it worked for her. What she said will give you a miniature view of how *Reasonably Thin* works, and works, and works.

"When I first came to see you, my whole focus was my weight. I was miserable and felt helpless to do anything about it. I had tried just about every diet in the book. Then we started working on the reasons why I ate destructively. I ate to self-nurture, because I didn't feel loved by my husband or family. I ate to calm my anxieties and loneliness. Like you said, I didn't have relationships with people. Food was my only relationship.

"You taught me about the real reason for food—for nourishment. So I determined to eat only for that reason. When I stopped eating for any reason other than nourishment, feelings began to emerge right and left. First there was anxiety, then fear, then deep sadness, and eventually anger. I still remember when you told me you thought I was angry, and I thought you were crazy. I didn't feel angry. But I didn't really feel much of anything. I used the food to numb out the feelings."

She went on. "I took each of the feelings and determined

where they came from. I felt anxious, because I had given up my way of numbing feelings, which was with food. I felt anxious because the problems I had been avoiding were starting to emerge. I felt fear because I was afraid to confront those problems. I felt sadness over the love I didn't feel from those around me. And then I felt anger over the same thing."

She continued. "Instead of running away from the feelings, I began to resolve them in the right ways. I openly and appropriately acknowledged my anger to my husband. He said he knew I was angry all along. I guess I was telling him without saying it. We talked many times about our relationship. We talked about things that needed to change, and we committed to work on them together. It was amazing. Dealing with my destructive eating properly led me into a deeper relationship with my husband and led both of us into deeper relationships with the Lord. Now, when I hurt, I can turn to the Lord and to my husband and get the nurturing I need." Corina looked out through eyes of deep satisfaction.

Reasonably Thin *is not really about a changed lifestyle. It is about living consistently with our new lives in Christ.*

"I worked through each of my feelings, talking to the Lord about them and turning to His Word on the issues. As I did, I gained in my knowledge of the Lord and in my closeness with Him. Because I had determined to face my unhappiness the right way, and not with food, I felt God's power instead of the power of my flesh. It was deep and satisfying.

It was in stark contrast to the shallow, temporary satisfaction of food."

She went on. "I began to look at all of my relationships and deal with each one of them honestly. Over that period of time, my entire life began to be cleansed of old stuff. Food began to be of little importance to me, and the desire to serve the Lord began to replace my fear of failure. I could stand the exposure now, because my life was what it was supposed to be. As you've said, 'Not perfect, but in progress.'"

Corina continued. "I used to think that surely there was something more waiting for me out there somewhere, some challenge that would take me where I wanted to go spiritually. But all the while I was looking beyond the challenge. It was right in front of me—it was food. I stopped seeing my eating behavior as something that made me bad or something that I just wanted to look away from. When I faced it, using the principles of *Reasonably Thin,* all of the rest fell into place."

"What do you mean?" I asked.

"When I looked at all of my reasons for my destructive eating, I began to correct much of my thinking. I was getting psychologically adjusted at the same time. When I corrected my thinking about food, I found that the same errors in thinking were also occurring elsewhere in my life. Like, thinking in extremes about food. I became aware that I thought in extremes in general. Because of that, my life tended to be an emotional roller coaster. Once I learned to think more according to the truth than in extremes, my life began to calm down. I began to mature emotionally. So did my relationships," Corina said.

"You've really come a long way," I said.

"That's right," Corina said, "all the way to being reasonably thin."

"Is being reasonably thin that important now?" I really wanted to know.

"Yes, and no," Corina said. "It's important for me to be reasonably thin. But as long as I'm obedient to the Lord in how I eat and how I live, being reasonably thin will be, as you said, the by-product. So I don't think much about it. I think mostly about what will bring Him glory. The rest will take care of itself!"

We shared smiles and tears as I have with others who have learned and applied the principles of *Reasonably Thin*.

Corina has moved on, but she will take with her and use the principles of *Reasonably Thin* in all of the other areas of her life. I am so grateful for God's Word and how specific it is to every area of our lives. *Reasonably Thin* is not really about a changed lifestyle. It is about living consistently with our new lives in Christ. We are victorious! When do we get to feel the victory experientially? The thrill of victory occurs at the point of knowing that you are exactly where God wants you to be and doing exactly what He wants you to do. There is no feeling like it in the world! It is the essence of freedom coupled with responsibility. The longer you stay there, the longer you live in the strong undercurrent of joy. It is a sense heightened only by the exhilarating and solid sense of purpose. What is the purpose? To live in such a way that God is revealed to the world through you. It is to glorify God. What is the price? Dealing with our pain.

Steps to Becoming Reasonably Thin

- Never cover pain. Choose to understand and move beyond it.

Prayer

Father, lead me to the other side of pain. I'm determined, in Your power, to live unencumbered. Thank You for this trial and all You will bring to me because of it. In the name of Jesus, amen.

37

Living Reasonably Thin

No one engaged in warfare entangles himself
with the affairs of this life, that he may please him
who enlisted him as a soldier.

—2 Timothy 2:4

If I were going to fight an alligator, it would probably be best that I not be preoccupied with something else at the time. The same would hold true for someone running a race in competition. Can you see an Olympic relay runner handing off the baton while she is putting tomorrow's agenda together or thinking about who is taking the children in to have their braces tightened? At times like these, the last thing anyone would want would be to be entangled with the things of this life. The reason for that is that the immediate goal requires full concentration. For those highly concentrated moments, all else moves into the background.

Winning that race affects every other area of the runner's

life. It builds self-esteem. It is a great model of discipline for others. It develops discipline that can be applied to other areas of life. It provides success to build upon.

That is the way it is with living reasonably thin. When we have learned that our goal in life is to bring glory to God, and that becomes our area of concentration, everything else falls into place. Because we insist on honoring God, our relationships are enhanced and fortified. Our emotional issues are brought to the surface for resolution. Our relationship with the Lord is more dear. Our faith is strengthened. Our destructive eating stops. And, our weight, which is no longer an object of concern, reverts to its healthy range.

> *When we have learned that our goal in life is to bring glory to God, and that becomes our area of concentration, everything else falls into place.*

In the process of learning to live reasonably thin, we have reclaimed our lives for Christ. Our minds are no longer entangled in the nightmare of destructive eating. There is joy where there used to be desperation, and calm where the storms of disappointment and self-hate used to rage. We are now free to be used to serve Christ in any capacity He should choose. There are no lead weights wrapped around our ankles as we run the race. Nothing encumbers us. Armed in Christ with truth, faith, and power, we will progress toward physical, emotional, psychological, and spiritual maturity. Our thinking, feeling, and behavior will have conformed to His mandates. In that God is glorified.

Some of what we have now may be new, such as freedom

from the willing bondage to food. The mirror is no longer our enemy. It is OK to go outside now, to socialize and enter friendships. It is OK to enjoy dinner, because it is safe and good. And we have learned to place in practice proper structures that protect us from ourselves.

> *The definition of success for the Christian is not that we reach a certain weight. The definition of success for the Christian is obedience.*

For some of us, we have reclaimed what once was lost: our comfort in our relationships with our spouses. Our zest for life. The light that used to shine unencumbered and brightly from within us, that once drew attention to Him rather than our struggle. Our self-esteem, based on who we are in Christ, is back. The joy of life is back.

It is time to celebrate! But what are we celebrating? Listen to Joshua: "This Book of the Law shall not depart from your mouth, but you shall meditate in it day and night, that you may observe to do according to all that is written in it. For then you will make your way prosperous, and then you will have good success" (Josh. 1:8).

The definition of success for the Christian is not that we reach a certain weight. The definition of success for the Christian is obedience. That is what we are celebrating. Bringing thoughts into captivity to obedience. It is not having reached a goal of perfection. Success is found in each and every instance of progress, each and every act of obedience. Now we must learn to repeat success, to continue progress! Listen to Paul talking about Noah in his letter to the

Hebrews: "By faith Noah, being divinely warned of things not yet seen, moved with godly fear, prepared an ark for the saving of his household, by which he condemned the world and became heir of the righteousness which is according to faith" (Heb. 11:7).

We might be tempted to think that Noah's success came at the point of launching the ark. But that was not the case. Every day, he cut another log or placed one log upon another. Each act was an act of obedience done in faith. Each day was a success. Each small action was no less significant than the next. His success was not based on the future. It was based on each act of obedience, here and now. That is the way it has to be, and can be with us too. We must never let a brief negative episode overshadow any success. Helen may represent many of us with her account of destructive eating.

Helen

"I'm so angry with myself and disappointed in myself!" That is how Helen started the conversation.

"Why are you angry and disappointed?" I asked.

"I was doing great until dinner. Then I ate more than I had planned to eat."

"What do you mean you were doing great?" I asked.

"I ate breakfast when and where I had planned. And I ate what I had planned. That's not how it usually goes for me. Then the same thing happened with lunch." Helen was ready to move on to her complaints about how she overate at dinner, but I stopped her.

"So you were successful today?" I suggested.

"Yes, but . . ." She was about to go on to her complaints again, but I interrupted.

"Actually you were successful more than once today?" I tried again.

"But . . ." Helen was determined to get her self-complaints back into the conversation. But I interrupted again.

"Wait a minute, you were successful in eating what, where, and when you had planned for breakfast and lunch. So you were actually successful at least six times today. At least you were six times successful in what you wanted to do. What about temptations to do what you hadn't planned to do? Were there any of those?" I still would not let her go back to the complaints.

"Yes," she said. "Someone offered me a doughnut when I was at the office. I thought about going across the street for a burger, instead of doing lunch as I had planned."

"OK, then let's add those in. That would be six successes for lunch and breakfast, plus resisting temptation twice. So that's eight successes. Are there any more?"

"I know two." Helen was catching on. "I overate at dinner, but I did eat where and when I had intended to!"

"Great!" She had gotten the idea. "That makes ten. You were successful at least ten times in one day. How does that compare with how you were doing when you started *Reasonably Thin*?"

"Are you kidding?" She chuckled. "There were no successes."

"So, you're extremely successful compared to how you used to be?" I asked.

"Yes," she said. "I hadn't looked at it that way."

"Now would you like to tell me about the incident at dinner?"

"Well, actually it wasn't such a big deal," she said.

"Good," I said. "Now you understand. If you fail to see the individual successes, the failures will always loom larger than they really are. You will then feel worse about yourself, emotional distress will set in, and that will be followed by the urge to eat destructively. The urge comes from wanting to find relief from the discomfort of failure."

Helen was making the mistake of focusing only on her failures. But, as you can see, that is a distorted perspective; it is not the whole truth. Once again, if you want to be reasonably thin, you will have to tell the entire truth. That is what Helen did!

Steps to Becoming Reasonably Thin

- Let your heart celebrate every single success, every single act of obedience. It honors God, brings Him glory, and releases joy in you.

Prayer

Father, thank You for forgiving me for failing to appreciate the successes You've given me and for focusing so much on the failures. I'm choosing joy now. I want You to be honored. I look to You for the power to obey and to celebrate what brings You glory! In the name of Jesus, amen.

Conclusion

And lest I should be exalted above measure by the abundance of the revelations, a thorn in the flesh was given to me, a messenger of Satan to buffet me, lest I be exalted above measure. Concerning this thing I pleaded with the Lord three times that it might depart from me. And He said to me, "My grace is sufficient for you, for My strength is made perfect in weakness." Therefore most gladly I will rather boast in my infirmities, that the power of Christ may rest upon me.

—2 Corinthians 12:7–9

Some people pray that God will remove their desire to overeat or to undereat. There is nothing at all wrong with doing that. But if God, as with Paul, does not remove that desire, He intends us to conquer it. He wants us to do that with His power and in cooperation with Him. He wants to use this trial for our growth and blessing. All of that results in His being glorified.

What God wants is for Christ to be made manifest to the world for which He died. That is done when we reveal who we really are! Who are we? What is our purpose here on this earth? Jesus explained it clearly, as recorded in Matthew 5:14–16: "You are the light of the world. A city that is set on a hill cannot be hidden. Nor do they light a lamp and put it under a basket, but on a lampstand, and it gives light to all who are in the house. Let your light so shine before men, that they may see your good works and glorify your Father in heaven."

> *Our lives are intended to encounter struggles, because Christ can be seen in them. That is where our faith moves from words to life.*

Our light is not to be hidden behind anything, including our weight. If we do not shine, how dark will this world be! Ours is not just a mandate, it is a divine privilege and responsibility to reveal to the world God's Son through whom He calls out to the world for reconciliation. Part of how God reveals Himself to the world is through our struggles with weight.

Our lives are intended to encounter struggles, because Christ can be seen in them. That is where our faith moves from words to life. If we turn to food to comfort ourselves in these difficult times, we forfeit this opportunity to apply God's Word to our lives. In this area, in this very struggle with weight, we forfeit living by faith. And to the degree that it affects any other area of our lives, we forfeit the God-given option of living, for Him, our highest and best. The choice is ours. As for me, I will not settle for less. Come join those of us who have chosen to live reasonably thin, because it honors Him! Our food is different now. It is, as Jesus said and John recorded in John 4:34, "to do the will of Him who sent Me, and to finish His work."

When all else is right with God, and you are making

choices about your life, always choose what will bring Him maximum glory! Settle for nothing less! How do we do that? Sow only things that bring Him glory! Listen to Paul in Galatians, and then again in 2 Corinthians: "Whatever a man sows, that he will also reap" (Gal. 6:7). "But this I say: He who sows sparingly will also reap sparingly, and he who sows bountifully will also reap bountifully" (2 Cor. 9:6).

Sow godly decisions about food, and you will reap growth, strengthened faith, and more. Your investment yields far greater than the original investment. God compounds the interest. You will grow spiritually, psychologically, and emotionally. Alongside your faith, you will move toward maturity. Sow godly decisions generously, and reap bountifully! That is how you bring Him maximum glory! Remember, inherent in every choice to honor God by eating reasonably is the certainty of bringing glory to God.

> *Sow godly decisions about food, and you will reap growth, strengthened faith, and more. Your investment yields far greater than the original investment. God compounds the interest.*

It is my prayer that you will return to *Reasonably Thin* as often as it in any way affords you answers on how to live a life that honors God.

Steps to Becoming Reasonably Thin

- Shine brightly for Him and those for whom He died.

Prayer

Father, etch into my heart that Your plan is always to be held higher than mine. Keep it clear in my mind that my goal in every area of my life is to bring You glory. Please bring these principles of Reasonably Thin *to my mind over and over until You are glorified in every area, including my eating behavior. Please conform my heart to the desire to bring You maximum glory and nothing less! Thank You, Father. In the name of Jesus, amen.*

How to Become a Christian

It may be that while reading this book you have felt the Lord tugging on your heart to come to Him. Let me give you this brief explanation of why we need Jesus Christ and how we may gain life in Him.

The Bible says that God is Spirit and righteous. It also says that man is spiritually dead and sinful. Our sin separates us from a relationship with God. We are unable to save ourselves and are in need of a savior. God sent His Son, Jesus Christ, to live the perfect life and to die for our sin and in our place. Jesus arose from the dead and now stands ready and able to save all who will come to Him. If you will come to Him, He promises He will give life.

Here is what the Bible says:

- "For all have sinned and fall short of the glory of God."
  —Romans 3:23
- "For the wages of sin is death, but the gift of God is eternal life in Christ Jesus our Lord."
  —Romans 6:23
- "But God demonstrates His own love toward us, in that while we were still sinners, Christ died for us."
  —Romans 5:8

261

- "That Christ died for our sins according to the Scriptures, and that He was buried, and that He rose again the third day according to the Scriptures."
  —1 Corinthians 15:3–4
- "For God so loved the world that He gave His only begotten Son, that whoever believes in Him should not perish but have everlasting life."
  —John 3:16

If you want to become a Christian, to be forgiven of your sin and gain eternal life, pray this prayer right now:

Lord, I want to know You. I believe that You died for me. I am asking You right now to come into my life, forgive me of my sin, and give me new life. I receive You as my Savior and Lord. Please take control of my life and make me the person You want me to be. I ask this in Jesus' name, amen.

If you have just prayed this prayer, you are now a Christian. I welcome you to the fellowship of Christians. Some people feel emotional at this moment, and others do not. Do not let that confuse you. It is not about how you feel, it is about the decision you made.

Now it is important for you to talk with others about your new life. It is important for you to join together with other Christians in learning more about this new life in Christ and what the Bible says about it and you. Take time today to call a church in your community and attend worship services this Sunday. Ask the church about a Bible study for new Christians, and then attend. Tell them that you are a new Christian. I was a new Christian once too. It was very important for me to enjoy fellowship with other Christians. It will be important for you too.

Go to a Christian bookstore and ask them to show you a Bible that would be best for someone who just became a Christian. Take it with you to church and to the Bible study for new Christians.

I would love to hear from you. Please feel free to write to me and let me know of your choice to accept Jesus Christ as your Savior. You may not know it now, but you just made the most important decision you will ever make in your life. I thank God for your salvation and for you.

About the Author

Every day, whether on her radio show, "Jesse Dillinger Live!" or in her private practice as a Marriage, Family, and Child Counselor, Jesse Dillinger observes how the lack of understanding and application of scriptural principles so profoundly and negatively affects people.

According to Jesse, "As Christians we cannot find in the world's frame of reference what will successfully guide and heal us. Only what God says and does, alongside our cooperation with Him, will have the result He wants and we want in our lives. It is a two-party transaction, and that is important to know. It is not just what God says that is important, but correspondingly what we do with what He says. This is my passion," says Jesse, "to be used of God to make the connection between those two truths so that our lives may so reflect Him as to draw others to His saving grace through His Son, Jesus Christ."

Her God-given insight into human behavior and her "bottom line approach" form the foundation of her successful practice in San Diego, California, where she focuses predominantly on Christians. There as on "Jesse Dillinger Live!" a talk show dealing with Christian relationships, the therapeutic approach is drawn from scriptural principles rather than secular psychology. Jesse brings these insights along with her deep love for God's Word and an occasional touch of humor into her writing and speaking, resulting in a dynamic and in-depth approach to the Word. You will find all of these ingredients in *Reasonably Thin*.